School of Divinity

Does it sometimes seem that God's promises apply to other believers, but not to you? In *Faith, Hope, and Love,* Charles L. Allen teaches you how you can realize the fulfillment of these promises in your life. His insights on such topics as unanswered prayer, forgiveness, humility, and effective prayer can help you to become a more obedient disciple of Christ. Let Charles L. Allen show you the way to a deeper *Faith, Hope, and Love* — and begin to experience the abundant life Jesus promises *all* believers.

FAITH, HOPE, and LOVE

Charles L. Allen

Fleming H. Revell Company
Old Tappan, New Jersey

Unless otherwise identified, Scripture quotations are from the King James Version of the Bible.

Scripture quotations identified MOFFATT are from THE BIBLE: A NEW TRANSLATION by James Moffatt. Copyright 1954 by James A. R. Moffatt. By permission of Harper & Row, Publishers, Inc.

Scripture quotations identified RSV are from the Revised Standard Version of the Bible, copyrighted 1946 and 1952.

Material in this volume from ROADS TO RADIANT LIVING copyright © 1951 by Fleming H. Revell Company.

Material in this volume from PRAYER CHANGES THINGS copyright © 1964 by Fleming H. Revell Company.

Material in this volume from THE MIRACLE OF HOPE copyright © 1973 by Fleming H. Revell Company.

Material in this volume from THE MIRACLE OF LOVE copyright © 1972 by Fleming H. Revell Company.

Quotation from *The Cocktail Party* by T. S. Eliot published by permission of Harcourt Brace Jovanovich, Inc.

Library of Congress Cataloging in Publication Data
Allen, Charles Livingstone, date
Faith, hope, and love.

1. Faith—Meditations. 2. Hope—Meditations. 3. Love (Theology)—Meditations.
I. Title.
BV4635.A44 241'.4 82-498
ISBN 0-8007-5096-9 (pbk.) AACR2

Contents

TO

Finis A. Crutchfield
Bishop of the United Methodist Church
Scholar—minister—Christian,
My Pastor

Preface
These Three

Through the years I have written on faith, on hope, on love, but Saint Paul reminds us that we should not and, in fact, cannot separate these. We all are so familiar with his words: "So faith, hope, love abide, these three . . ." (1 Corinthians 13:13 RSV). As I read that sentence, I underscore the words "these three." So I wanted to bring together into one volume some of the best insights I have had through the years on these topics. I appreciate very much my publisher permitting me to use material from previous writings in order to help me to accomplish the bringing together of "these three."

Without any doubt, these are the most important human expressions, and they should be considered together.

To begin with I want to underscore the word *abide.* It is a strong, sturdy word. One of the joys I have is leading groups on tours of the Holy Land. I intend to continue doing that at least three times a year. To me, it is a thrillingly exciting experience. In the Holy Land one of the places that we like to visit is Emmaus. Very few tours go there, but I always insist on it because it means so much to Christian people. The most beautiful view in all of Israel can be seen from Emmaus. There we remember our Lord's appearance on Sunday afternoon of His resurrection. One of the things about Emmaus is that it was there that Henry Francis Lyle wrote the wonderful hymn, "Abide With Me." I always have our group sing the first verse of that hymn, which closes with these words:

When other helpers fail and comforts flee,
Help of the helpless, O abide with me.

So many of the things that we seek the most are only temporary—clothes that go out of style, cars that wear out, treasures that "moth and rust doth corrupt." Often the joy of material blessings is overshadowed by the realization that someday they will be lost. Physical strength will become weakness; the years will steal away physical beauty; the most brilliant career will come to an end; thunderous applause will die into silence.

But there are "three things" within our reach that will "abide": faith, hope, love.

Faith Abides

Without faith we are not sure of ourselves: we find decisions difficult to make; we are afraid to dare, to dream, to adventure.

When Admiral Du Pont was explaining to Admiral Farragut the reasons why he failed to enter Charleston Harbor with his fleet of ironclads, Farragut listened until he was through and said, "Du Pont, there is one reason more why you failed." "What is that?" Du Pont asked. Farragut's answer was, "You did not believe that you could do it."

Failing to possess faith ends in dreary failures.

What is faith? Essentially it means two things: First, it means to continue to believe in certain truths, no matter what happens. One of the grandest statements that Saint Paul ever made was, ". . . I have kept the faith" (2 Timothy 4:7). Life dealt harshly with him, but through it all he never gave up, and he never quit.

The other part of faith is, that when we face up to life situations that we know we are unable to handle, we depend on a higher help. In this connection, faith means three things about God: (1) God created the world. That means that at the very heart of things are the principles of God. For a time it may seem that evil will triumph, but let us remember that He said, "I am the Alpha and the Omega, the beginning and the ending . . ."

(Revelation 1:8). God was the beginning, and we can be sure God will be the end.

(2) Faith means that God cares. At times one feels forgotten and deserted, but remembering there is somebody who hasn't deserted us gives inspiration and courage.

(3) Faith means God is working with us and not just watching us from afar. God did not create the world and leave it. He is still here and we sing together:

> This is my Father's world,
> O let me ne'er forget
> That though the wrong seems oft so strong
> God is the Ruler yet.
>
> MALTBIE D. BABCOCK

Faith will continue to live on. We talk about "losing faith." The truth is, no person ever loses faith. We just quit using our faith.

Hope Abides

Hope is a big, strong word, and it should never be watered down to represent mere wishful thinking. Hope is a firm expectation, based on certain fundamental truths and actions. It is never a substitute for clear thinking or hard work. On the contrary, it is the inspiration both to thinking and to working.

It has been pointed out that profanity is not the "swear words" that people use. Those words are more stupid than sinful. The most profane word is the word, *hopeless.* The Psalmist said, ". . . hope thou in God . . ." (Psalms 42:5).

The word *hopeless* denies the existence of God. To *hope* is to affirm our faith in God.

When one becomes discouraged and the future seems utterly dark, there are three actions he can take. (1) There is the way of the fool: "The fool hath said in his heart, There is no God"

(Psalms 14:1). The fool has no place to turn for support when things go wrong. The only thing to do is to give up and quit.

(2) There is the cynic's way of looking at the troubles of life. This is a little better than the way of the fool, but not much. The cynic believes that everything turns out badly. "This is just my luck," is the philosophy of the cynic. The cynic maybe doesn't quit, but just suffers through existence, not expecting much and blundering through life.

(3) The third way to face life is the way of hope. There will be disappointments, setbacks, but hope sees the sunshine behind the clouds. Hope remembers that God gave us ears to hear the music because there will always be music to hear. Hope believes God gave us eyes to see beauty because there will always be beauty to see. Hope knows that in spite of the hurts of life, we keep going to better experiences ahead.

So Hope, Faith, Love Abide, These Three

The three must go together. Love is the climax. It is the "end of the rainbow."

We need to remind ourselves that this statement of Saint Paul, "So faith, hope, love abide, these three; but the greatest of these is love," is the climax of the thirteenth chapter of 1 Corinthians (RSV). This chapter is Saint Paul's inspired explanation of love. We know that sunlight can shine through a prism and be broken down to its many colors. The great Henry Drummond showed us how Saint Paul let love shine through the prism of his brilliant mind, and love was broken down into its many component parts. In this chapter he explained what love is. He analyzes love for us. There has never been a more complete statement on the meaning of love and its varied expressions in life than the thirteenth chapter of 1 Corinthians.

In the following pages are some of the thoughts that I have had through my years about faith, hope, and love.

CHARLES L. ALLEN
First United Methodist Church
Houston, Texas

PART I

FAITH

1
Use Your Faith

One of the things we need most is faith. Some people feel that faith is silly and put it in the same category as fairies, something beautiful but unreal. Actually, faith is the most practical, down-to-earth thing we possess, and we all possess it. Without faith one could not live a day.

I got up this morning and pressed the light switch—I had faith that the electricity would come through. I turned on the faucet and took a drink of water—I had faith that the city authorities had made it fit for drinking, so I did not analyze it myself. My wife could have put poison in my breakfast (and I suspect sometimes she is tempted to do so), but I had faith in her, so I ate it without question. I stepped on the starter of my car because I had faith in the battery. When I stopped at the filling station to get ten gallons of gas I did not measure it myself, because I had faith in the attendant.

I deposit my money in the bank because I have faith. I buy a bond that will not mature for ten years, but I do it because I have faith. I mailed my premium on an insurance policy. I do not know the officers of the company, have never seen them, but I send them money because I have faith in them. In the very act of mailing a letter I am exercising faith in the many postal employees who will handle it. I get on an elevator and ride up several stories because I have faith that it will not fall.

I go to the doctor because I have faith in him. I know

nothing about the medicine he gives me, but my faith causes me to take it. I walk down the street without fear because I have faith in the people I meet and do not believe they would shoot me in the back. I plant seed in the ground because of my faith that they will germinate and come up, and then I have faith that the sun will shine and the rain will fall in sufficient amounts to make the seed grow. I work for my employer because I have faith that I will be paid at the proper time. I trust part of my work to other people because of my faith that they will do the work conscientiously and well.

I undertake some job that I have never done before, but I have faith that it can be done. I could enumerate examples for several pages, because there is hardly an act of my life that does not exercise faith. We all use it.

But when it comes to the biggest and most important thing of my life, my relationship with God, it is so easy to say that faith is all bunk, to say, "I don't have anything to do with this religious business. I want something real and practical."

The author of Hebrews reminds us, "Without faith it is impossible to please God" (11:6), and we might add ourselves or anyone else. Without faith life is unlivable. If you would build a great character you must first build a great faith. And really it is a very easy thing to have faith. In fact, you cannot help but have faith. You could no more quit having faith than you could quit breathing.

The definition for faith that we find in Hebrews is as good as any, "Faith is . . . the evidence of things not seen" (11:1). Close your eyes for a moment. Now, with them closed, you can see this printed page. Look now and you can actually see the door to your church, the pulpit inside your church. Look again and you can see your schoolroom, the soda fountain in the drug store, the face of your best friend. In fact, by looking through your mind's eye, you can see a thousand times as much as you can see through your physical eyes. And that is faith.

This very moment you can actually see Jesus. Look at Him as He feeds the multitude, or as He talks to Zacchaeus sitting in the tree, or as He calls the Rich Young Ruler. Right now you can see Him hanging on the cross. Suggest any scene of His life, and you can see it through your mind's eye. And that is faith.

Here is a boy struggling through school. The work is hard and he has to make some sacrifice to keep going. Why does he stick to it? Simply because he sees himself as a man taking his rightful place in the world because he is prepared. From that mental picture of himself several years in the future he gains inspiration and courage. And that is faith.

Jesus said, "I go to prepare a place for you." Immediately there flashes on the screen of your mind a picture of that place, and you see life after death. And that is faith.

With these same mental eyes we see God. He does not have to be here in the flesh. And the more you are in contact with Him through worship and study and meditation, the clearer your picture of Him becomes. Look right now. Do you not see God? And that is faith.

So we understand exactly what the author of Hebrews meant when he said of Moses, "He endured, as seeing him who is invisible" (11:27). Open your mind and heart and let your own mental sight (or faith) lead you to the highest things of life.

2
Five Questions About Prayer

Often people write or speak to me of problems for which I just do not know the answers. In such cases I admit that I do not know how to advise him or her, but I suggest that we enter into a compact together to pray about it. Many times, as a result of our prayers, problems have been solved.

One man, however, in response to my prayer suggestion, wrote back a very difficult letter. "Before I agree to pray," he wrote, "answer the following five questions: What is prayer? Can anybody pray? Can you prove the value of prayer? How does one pray? What results can I expect from prayer?" How would you answer those questions? Let's take them one at a time:

WHAT IS PRAYER?

What is prayer? In a very fine speech which I heard one night, a scientist was explaining the difference between "black magic" and "white magic." Black magic is using the forces of evil for one's own benefit. White magic is using the forces of good for one's own benefit. He went on to explain that many people think of religion as something they can use. Many people think of prayer merely as white magic.

Prayer is not magic. Prayer is within the laws of the universe, and the spiritual laws of the universe are as certain and sure as are the physical laws. Physical and spiritual laws work together; they are never in conflict. As Pierhal states it, "Although prayer is supernatural, it is not anti-natural."

Prayer is never a substitute for effort. A certain schoolboy failed in his examinations. He was very much surprised. When the teacher inquired how much he had studied, he replied, "I did not study at all. I thought that if you asked God to help you, that was all you had to do."

On the other hand, prayer is something beyond our efforts. On the night of July 10, 1943, General Dwight D. Eisenhower watched the vast armada of 3,000 ships sailing across from Malta to the shores of Sicily for a great battle. The general saluted his heroic men and then bowed his head in prayer. To an officer beside him, Eisenhower explained, "There comes a time when you've used your brains, your training, your technical skill, and the die is cast and the events are in the hands of God, and there you have to leave them."

Prayer is need finding a voice—embarrassment seeking relief—a friend in search of a Friend—knocking on a barred door—reaching out through the darkness. Prayer is speaking, or thinking, or feeling with the belief that there is Somebody who hears and who cares and who will respond. Prayer is a means of contact with God. Prayer is opening our lives to the purposes of God.

Prayer is not a method of using God; rather is prayer a means of reporting for duty to God.

CAN ANYBODY PRAY?

Can anybody pray? The answer is, Everybody can and does pray. Some people think they are self-sufficient and do not need help. Some people scoff at the value of prayer, calling it a silly waste of time. Some people lack faith; others are ashamed to face God in prayer because of some sin; some are afraid to pray because they do not want God telling them what to do.

But at one time or another, in one kind of crisis or another, everybody prays. Need becomes stronger than doubt and sometimes we will turn to God in spite of ourselves. There is a hidden hunger of man's spiritual self that cries out to be satisfied. Sooner or later that hidden hunger asserts itself and makes its demands felt. It is as Victor Hugo said, "There are times in a man's life when, regardless of the attitude of the body, the soul is on its knees in prayer."

CAN YOU PROVE THE VALUE OF PRAYER?

Can you prove the value of prayer? By various tests, many have sought to demonstrate that prayer gets results. But I have never been too interested in such experiments. I am not sure that prayer values can be proved, but certainly they can be known. There is a difference. In fact, anyone who sincerely prays is himself a proof of prayer.

About prayer, Lincoln once said: "I have had so many evidences of His direction, so many instances of times when I have been controlled by some other power than my own will, that I cannot doubt that this power comes from God. I frequently see my way clear to a decision when I am conscious that I have not sufficient facts on which to found it. I am satisfied that, when the Almighty wants me to do, or not to do, a particular thing, He finds a way of letting me know. I talk to God and when I do my mind seems relieved and a way is suggested." I doubt if Lincoln ever tried to prove the value of prayer—but he knew it.

HOW DOES ONE PRAY?

How does one pray? Late one night my doorbell rang. When I opened the door I found a man standing there. He said, "Something happened to me tonight that caused me to want to pray. But I have never prayed in my life and I do not know how. I don't want you to pray for me—I want you to teach me how to pray for myself." We talked for a while and I found he had never been to church except for a few times when he was a child. He had never read the Bible. I asked if he knew the Lord's Prayer. He asked, "What is that?"

I told him about Jesus' disciples asking Him to teach them to pray. In response, He gave them a short prayer. I gave my visitor a New Testament and marked the place. I told him that every time he wanted to pray he should get down on his knees, open the Testament, and read that prayer aloud. He said he would do that, and he was deeply in earnest. As a result, that man had a really remarkable religious experience and has developed a wonderful faith.

The best way I know to learn to pray is to learn the Lord's Prayer by heart. It is easy to commit the Lord's Prayer to memory; it takes time and persistence to learn it by heart. But when those words that Jesus gave come out of our own hearts, then we are truly praying.

WHAT RESULTS CAN I EXPECT FROM PRAYER?

What results can I expect from prayer? Some years ago four people who knew much about prayer joined together in forming a declaration. They were George Washington Carver, Glenn Frank, Rufus Jones, and Muriel Lester. They wrote:

Sometimes a bridge falls, but that does not mean that the law of gravity has failed. Sometimes lines are short-circuited, but that does not mean that the law of electricity has failed. And sometimes a disciple betrays his Lord, but that does not mean that the law of love has failed. Sometimes a prayer is not answered, but that does not mean that the power of prayer has failed. The scientist does not quit when the lights are short-circuited, nor when the bridge falls. Then why should we? Just think of what would happen if all church people united in prayer with as great faith in the laws of God as scientists have in the laws of nature.

Science is showing us that the smaller and more invisible a thing is, the more powerful it is. Pasteur proved to an unbelieving world that bacteria ten thousand times smaller than a flea could kill a man. Physicists are proving that the tiny cosmic ray is far more potent and penetrating than the visible sun ray. Radio operators are proving that the short-wave length carries a message farther than the long-wave length. And love is invisible, but all-powerful love is more potent and penetrating than cannons, submarines or airplanes ever can be. Prayer in the inner room, invisible to the eyes of men, is still as potent as in the days when Jesus said, "Pray to thy Father who is in secret and thy Father who seeth in secret shall reward you openly."

George Meredith said, "Who riseth from prayer a better man, his prayer is answered." That is really the best result of prayer, but prayer brings definite and tangible results. However, we must keep in mind that we ourselves must become part of the answer.

Here is an illustration: A poor man who lived in the country had an accident and broke his leg. That meant he was laid up for a long while, unable to work. His family was large and needed help. Someone got up a prayer meeting at the church to pray for this family. While the people were praying and asking God to help the family, there was a loud knock on the door of their home. Someone tiptoed to the door, opened it, and there stood a young farm boy who said, "My dad could not attend the prayer meeting tonight, so he just sent his prayers in a wagon." And there was the wagon loaded with potatoes, meat, apples, and other things from the farm. There was an instance where prayers were loaded in a wagon.

As I said, we must become part of the answer to our prayers, but only part. God adds to our abilities, opportunities, and resources whatever is needed and is right to bring about the full answer. It is as Tennyson said,

> More things are wrought by prayer
> Than this world dreams of. . . .

3

Learn to Pray

The lights were burning, the janitor was running the vacuum cleaner, and the organist was playing a beautiful melody as I walked into my church one morning. Into the building some wires run, over which flows that marvelous power that gives light, that cleans up and produces harmony.

Now, the God who created electricity did not forget to create a power that will do those same things for a life. And the channel through which that power flows is what we call prayer. The disciples once said to Christ, "Lord, teach us to pray." It is the only thing they ever asked Him to teach them. They knew that, once they learned to pray, the power of God was at their disposal.

In response to that request, Christ gave them seven simple steps to follow. He needed only sixty-six words (Matthew 6:9–13), and the power is available to any who follow those steps.

(1) Start by thinking of God. Forget about your own needs and problems for the time being and saturate your mind with thoughts of God. This will silence the mind and bring relaxation. Think of Him as "Our Father which art in heaven." You cannot imagine a cyclone in heaven. Heaven suggests calmness, beauty, and rest. Note the first word is "Our." You cannot pray for yourself alone.

(2) Then let your prayer begin with thanking God for

what He has done for you. Think of some definite blessings you have received and "name them one by one." You cannot hope to name them all, but do name some. This leads to positive and constructive thinking. It tends to diminish our bitterness, disappointment, and defeatist attitudes. "Hallowed be Thy name."

(3) Naturally, the next step is consecration—"Thy kingdom come, thy will be done." As we think of the benefits we have received from God, we want Him more and more in our lives and in our world. We realize that it is better for us to have God, and we increasingly want Him to have full possession of us. Possessing us, we want to help Him possess the world about us.

So we pray that God will use us in His work. We begin to see things we might do to help, and we gladly commit ourself to those opportunities. Anything that we can do to bring His kingdom in we eagerly become willing to do.

(4) As you realize the greatness of God, you understand that all we have comes from His hand. That if God stopped giving for even one minute, every bit of life on earth would cease. We think of our complete dependence on Him. So we pray, "Give us this day our daily bread."

> Back of the loaf is the snowy flour, and back of the flour is the mill;
> And back of the mill is the sheaf, and the shower and the sun, and the Father's will.

(5) Then, when we realize that wrong within our own lives blocks out our ability to serve and also feel our utter dependence on God, confession comes next. "Forgive us our sins" is the fifth step.

Here we need to be specific. In dealing with many people,

I have come to see that it is usually some definite wrong that needs to be settled. When we become willing to turn loose "that one thing," we usually have little difficulty in settling all the other things that are wrong.

(6) As we seek forgiveness of our own sins we are simultaneously seeking the forgiveness of every other person. Because as God comes into our own hearts there also comes in a deep and abiding love for Him and for all other people.

Here we feel the "expulsive power of a new affection." Prejudice, jealousy, hate, grudges, and indifference cannot live in a heart into which God has come. Thus it is easy and natural to pray, "As we forgive others."

(7) Finally comes the most important step of all. It is "Amen." That is a big and strong word. Literally, it means, "So let it be." It is a resolve of honesty. Obviously it would be dishonest and unfair to ask God to do for us what we are unwilling to do for ourselves. That word, "Amen," is a promise that you will do all within your own power to answer your prayer.

Also, "Amen" means what Jesus meant when He said, "Into thy hands I commend my spirit." That is, I have done my best and now I am willing to leave the results to God. It is a pledge of faith and confidence. Thus, when one has prayed, his mind can be at rest in the assurance that God has heard and will answer.

Those seven simple steps are the "how of prayer," and when honestly taken, they become the pathway to power—power that gives light and understanding, a clean heart, and harmony within the soul.

4

Learn to Believe

One of my favorite stories is found in the ninth chapter of Mark. A father had brought his sick son to the disciples of Jesus to be healed but they had failed to heal him. The father had about lost hope.

Then Jesus came up and said, "If thou canst believe, all things are possible to him that believeth." The father replied, "Lord, I believe."

And to those of us who are defeated, worried, anxious, and afraid, Jesus is saying it is possible for us to succeed if we will only learn how to believe.

This principle has been proved time and again. Take football for example. The greatest football coach of all time was Knute Rockne. One of his first rules for the selection of players on his Notre Dame teams was this: "I will not have a boy with an inferiority complex. He must believe he can accomplish things."

William James, the famous psychologist, said the same thing. He said, "Our belief at the beginning of a doubtful undertaking is the one thing that assures the successful outcome of any venture." Notice he says, "the one thing."

If any person expects to succeed, he must first learn to believe. I say learn to believe because it must be learned. We had to learn how to walk. Before we learned, we probably fell many times, but we can walk now because we kept on trying after each fall.

Now, there are some simple steps that can lead one to the tremendous power of belief. It is not easy to learn, but as we learn we will see the magic of belief working marvelous transformations in our lives.

Notice that Jesus says, "All things are possible." That is the first step. Eliminate the word "impossible" from your vocabulary.

I have hanging on the wall of my study a large card with these words: "CERTAINLY IT CAN BE DONE." I see it every day and I know what it can do for a person. I wish I could put that card where every person could see it every day.

Someone has suggested a simple technique that I have tried and know will work. Start Monday morning and keep a careful record of the times you say or think that anything is impossible. Just before you go to bed write the number down.

On Tuesday concentrate on reducing the number of times you say or think something cannot be done. Write that number down Tuesday night. Keep that up every day, and by the end of the week you will have made marvelous progress toward completely eliminating negative thoughts from your mind.

In the church of which I am pastor, we often sing a little chorus that has become a great help to a lot of us. I find myself singing it to myself as I go about my daily work. It goes like this: "Only believe, only believe all things are possible; only believe."

Second, when you get those old negative impossibles out of your mind you will slowly and hesitantly begin saying and thinking, "Lord, I believe." It won't be easy, because your mind will slyly say to you, "Don't bother with such silly ideas. It might help some people but it won't work for you."

But no matter what your doubtful mind says, just keep saying firmly and persistently, "Lord, I believe," and gradually the very pattern of your thoughts will become patterns of faith.

However, many fail because they miss the most important part. This man did not say to Jesus, "I believe." He said, "Lord, I believe." There is a tremendous difference here.

Here is the place psychology or psychiatry alone falls down. You cannot do it by yourself. The Christian faith uses all the principles and techniques of psychology and psychiatry, but it has so much more.

At the very center of the Christian faith is an eternal, all-powerful God. When one starts with God, putting his belief first in Him, it makes the major difference. You cannot do it by yourself, but with His help you can eventually really know what Saint Paul meant when he said, "I can do all things through Christ which strengtheneth me (Philippians 4:13).

There are a lot of people who are defeated in some way. They are harassed by a feeling of futility and helplessness. But as the sun breaks through the clouds, bringing light and warmth to the earth, so this simple faith will drive the clouds out of your life and make you happy and victorious.

"All things are possible to him that believeth—Lord, I believe" (Mark 9:23, 24).

5
Believe in Something Big

I talk to people every week whose lives are tangled, and for whom living is a hard experience. Not in every case but certainly in a lot of cases the trouble is that they do not believe in anything. As the result of talking with so many people, Mark 9:23, "All things are possible to him that believeth," has become my favorite text.

Strong beliefs are to a life what roots are to a mighty oak tree. Fierce winds may blow, but the oak stands because it has roots to hold it firm and secure. The person who does not have strong beliefs cannot expect to cope with the adversities of life. So I spend a lot of time trying to fix belief in the mind of people who come to see me as minister and counselor.

There are many things on which I have opinions and notions, but the seven listed below are the convictions of my heart. They are my own beliefs:

(1) I believe in THE BIBLE. I list that first because it is the most thorough and reliable source of our knowledge of God. I know that the Bible is a progressive revelation of God and that it must be interpreted in the light of the day in which it was written.

There are some regulations and customs in the Bible that do not apply to us today. For example, Abraham had authority to take the life of his son Isaac. But the Bible sets forth the eternal principles of life, and they are as new today as they were thousands of years ago.

(2) I believe in GOD. He is the all-powerful creator and controller of this universe. There is nothing weak or flabby about Him. He is holy, perfectly good, and so He abhors evil. There is no instance in which He can compromise between right and wrong; neither can He permit me to do it.

He is a personal Father and I am His child. He knows my name, the thoughts of my mind, and the desires of my heart. He will help me in every way that I will let Him. The Psalmist said, "He healeth the broken in heart. . . . He telleth the number of the stars" (Psalms 147:3, 4). That is, the God who created this universe is a power available to me personally.

(3) I believe in JESUS CHRIST. He once lived on this earth. He lived a perfect life, and He so thoroughly understood the spiritual laws of the universe that He could work miracles. "Even the winds and the sea obey him" (Matthew 8:27). He could heal the sick and even raise the dead.

He was more than a man. He was the divine Son and the Saviour of the world. His death on the cross is the only doorway for my soul into salvation. He rose again from the dead.

(4) I believe in PERSONAL SALVATION. It may come in a moment's flash, as it came to Saint Paul. Or it may come as a steady growth, as it came to Timothy. Or it may come in a quiet decision, as it came to Zacchaeus. But there is such a thing as a person being "saved."

I have a free will and I can accept and reject it, but I do know salvation is offered to me and to every person, no matter who he is or what he has done.

(5) I believe in the KINGDOM OF GOD ON EARTH. This is a belief that God is stronger than Satan, that love is

stronger than hate, that goodness is stronger than evil. I have no sympathy with the doctrine that the world is getting worse. I am convinced that when I line up on God's side I am on the winning side. The tide of His kingdom is on the way in.

(6) I believe in the CHURCH. It is not just another organization started and controlled by men. The church was born in the heart of God, and today it is sustained by His mighty power. Beyond any lodge or club, the church must have my first allegiance, and I do not begrudge one ounce of my strength, one moment of my time, or one cent of my money that I give to God's church.

I believe in the church prophetic, the church that has a message of authority and that bows to no state or ruler; in the church of worship, that instills the spirit of reverence in the hearts of men; in the church of service; and in the church that is to be, that will one day lift men above all divisions into one great fellowship of love.

(7) I believe in ETERNAL LIFE, that the short span of years on this earth is merely a fleeting introduction to the next life God has prepared. Beyond this life there is a judgment, and some day I will have to face up to the way I have lived here.

There is a heaven and there is a hell. It is possible for me to live my life here and refuse to think of God and His claims on me. But every act of my life has an eternal significance. The sorrows, injustices, and hardships in this life will be compensated for in the next. The unforgiven sins in this life will be paid for in the next. I believe I will never die.

These are the convictions of my own life. What do *you* believe?

6
Steps to Forgiveness

I stuck a splinter in my finger. It was not a big splinter but I took careful pains to get it out. I knew there was the possibility of that splinter setting up an infection. And, if let alone, that infection could go up my arm and through my body, and even could kill me.

Now, the human mind is a lot like the body. The mind can be wounded. Things can get into the mind that will set up an infection that can destroy a life.

Sorrow is a wound. But sorrow is a clean wound and, unless something gets into sorrow like self-pity, bitterness, and so on, the mind wounded by sorrow will heal.

Sin is a wound. But sin is an unclean wound, and unless it is removed from the mind, it will never heal. Instead, it will go out over your nervous system and make you jumpy and jittery. It will go to your heart and accelerate its action. It will go to your stomach and upset your digestion. Sin is the wrecker of more lives than any other disease.

When I do something that violates my standards of right and wrong, I have put an unclean thing into my mind. It may not be a very big thing, and like the splinter in my finger, it may seem not to amount to much, yet even a very small wrong can set up an infection within my mind.

A very prominent physician said to me only recently that many of his patients did not need to see him. They needed to see a minister who could help them cleanse their consciences.

Instead of sleeping pills, a lot of people need an old-fashioned period of repentance. Instead of a new drug, a lot of us need an experience of forgiveness. We need to get right with God and with our own consciences.

A person cannot do wrong and get by with it. You cannot stick a splinter in your finger and just ignore it. It must be removed. The same is true of a wrong in the mind.

Time and again, I have prescribed to people the Fifty-first Psalm. It is David's prayer of repentance.

David had done wrong. He had reached the point where he could not continue to live with himself.

In that prayer he prays, "Have mercy upon me, O God." Justice is not enough. Only through God's mercy is forgiveness possible.

"I acknowledge my transgressions." He does not tell God he is no worse than somebody else. He pleads no mitigating circumstances. He frankly admits he has done wrong.

"Wash me, and I shall be whiter than snow." He has faith that forgiveness is possible. He believes that no person is hopeless in the hands of the Great Physician.

"Create within me a clean heart." He wants to be guilty no more. He is willing to change his way of living.

"Restore unto me the joy of thy salvation." He recognizes that happiness is possible only to one in a right relationship with God.

"Then will I teach transgressors thy ways." If he is healed he promises not to be ashamed of the physician. He will tell others.

Those were the steps that David took after he had committed terrible sins, even murder. And they led him to the place where, later, he could say, "The Lord is my shepherd; I shall not want."

It worked for David. I have seen those very same steps work wonders in the lives of many, many people.

Some time ago Mary Pickford wrote a little book, the title of which was, "Why Not Try God?" Well, why not? We have tried nearly everything else, and a lot of us are still miserable and unhappy.

I said that to a person not long ago and his reply was, "I have so completely neglected God that now I am ashamed to face Him."

I asked him whether he would be ashamed to face his physician if he were sick? Or whether he would be ashamed to face his mechanic if his car broke down?

Then why be ashamed to face Him who loves us completely and who can always heal?

Indeed, why not try God?

7

We Can Get the Forgiveness Feeling

In the Lord's Prayer we pray, "... forgive us our debts ..." (Matthew 6:12). Instead of saying "debts," many use the word "transgressions," or "sins," but the word "debt" has vivid meaning for most of us. Debt can be a terrible burden; to know that all your debts are paid in full is a glorious experience.

As I went through college I had to borrow some money to help pay the expenses; so when I started preaching, I was in debt. I was required to make a payment each month on what I owed. I had an old car, but it finally wore out completely and I traded it in for a new one. I signed a contract to pay so much a month until it was paid for. Paying for that car is where I got my best idea of eternity.

I remember some of the letters the finance company wrote when I got behind on my car payments. They were fearful! Once, when I got two months behind, a man came after the car. I never talked so fast in my life! If I could preach as well as I talked to that man, I would make a lot of converts.

In those years we didn't have to have many clothes, but we had to buy some along the way. It was illegal to go without clothes. But what we bought were always on the installment plan. I remember an overcoat I bought for five dollars down and five dollars a month. I missed so many payments that by the time I finally made the last one, the coat was worn threadbare. We even bought our groceries on credit. My limited credit at the grocery store is one reason why I am so skinny today.

In those years it took every dollar I got to pay for something I had already eaten up or worn out. It worried me to be in debt. I don't remember asking God to let those debts be "forgiven," but I did pray many times asking God to show me how to make enough money to pay up everything.

We worked hard, the Lord helped us, and finally there came a day when all our debts were paid. There were no more mean letters about our payments being behind, and what money we had was clear and free. A great burden was lifted from my mind, and I felt new joy and happiness.

But debts for cars and clothes and other things are not the worst ones. How about the burden of debt that comes because of our sins against God? How can we ever feel that debt is paid?

Most of us know the burden of being in debt. I used to trade with a grocerman who kept his accounts in a big book. I would pay him as I could and he would mark "paid" by certain items; but the trouble was that I had to keep on eating, so I would charge other things. It was hard to get that page completely paid off.

As children we got the idea that God kept a list of our sins in a big book. Each of those sins was like a debt we owed and would have to pay. Some of our sins we felt we could pay by doing something really good. Sometimes, when trouble or misfortune came, we felt God was making us pay in that way. We never could catch up because we would do other things that were bad and they would be recorded against us.

Finally we come to the place where we feel we can never

pay off our debt of sin to God. We feel hopelessly doomed. Then we remember that Jesus taught us to pray, "... forgive us our debts...." Will God answer that prayer? Can we know that our page in God's book is marked "Paid in Full"? Can we really feel forgiven? We can if we will accept six facts—not only in our minds, but also in our hearts:

(1) God wants to forgive us; He loves us and understands us. The Bible tells us, "If we confess our sins, he is faithful and just to forgive us our sins ..." (1 John 1:9). Why confess? God already knows all about us. Confession is our recognition that what we have done is wrong; it also means our desire to have it taken out of our lives and hearts. We do not need to persuade God to forgive. As we look at the cross we realize that He loves us and goes to the uttermost for us.

(2) Forgiveness means that we are again on good terms with God. It does not take away the memory of our wrongs; the pain and sorrow of our failures will always remain with us. Neither does forgiveness take away all the consequences of our sins; some of our sins we will pay for until we die. But forgiveness does mean that a right relationship with God is restored. We can again respond to His love. His power and peace can flow freely into our hearts. We do not feel cut off and alone. We feel in our hearts that He is our Father and we are His children.

(3) God does not expect us to rid ourselves of our sins. The old song has it right: "Just as I am, ... I come, I come!" God is not some tyrant who takes delight in making us feel condemned and who wants to whip us. I once had a schoolteacher who seemed to get real joy out of using a big leather strap. I was so afraid of him I never learned much in his class. God is not like that. He says, "I know what is troubling you. I don't expect you to conquer all the evil thoughts

and desires in your heart. But come and let Me help you and together we will find the right way. I will walk with you to guide and strengthen and help you find joy and satisfaction."

(4) When forgiven, we can go on. God expects that. He doesn't want us to keep on confessing the same sin. He doesn't want us to keep chewing over the past. When Jesus says that God is a Father, that helps me because I had an earthly father who was like what I want to believe God is. One of papa's rules with his children was to settle whatever wrong we had done before we went to bed. If we needed talking to, he never put it off until tomorrow. After the matter was settled he never mentioned it again, nor would he permit us to.

God is a Father who settles things. Forgiveness means that we have been set free to go on living, and God expects us to go on. Face it, settle it, go on—that is the way to deal with sin before God.

(5) Forgiveness means that we surrender a wrong, and we surrender to God. Why do we do something that is wrong? Because we can't help it? No, because we don't want to help it. We do wrong things because we enjoy them or because we profit by them. As long as the joy we receive from wrong is greater than the joy of a right relationship with God, we shall keep on. But when we decide, truly decide, that we want God more than that wrong, then we are willing to give it up.

Also, we cannot say to God, "I am Yours, but on my terms." Again and again have I talked with someone in regard to making his life right with God. Often one has replied, "But I am not sure about what God wants me to do." My reply is, "Completely decide that you will do the right thing. Then, when you have committed yourself, God will show you what the right thing is." God gives insight to those who trust Him.

(6) If we do not feel forgiven, it is probably because of our own pride. It is so easy to tell ourselves, "I'm not such a bad fellow. I really don't need any help." We think of many good things we have done. We list the better qualities of our lives. Then we remind ourselves of the mean things other people do that we haven't done. We decide we can get along without God's forgiveness. But such talk is only pretending; we know that we are guilty and that we cannot save ourselves. It takes a strong man to get on his knees before God.

In *Pilgrim's Progress,* we recall how Christian was making his way toward the Eternal City. On his back was the burden of his sins. He came to Calvary, climbed to the top, and knelt at the cross. The sins were loosed, rolled down the hill into a sepulcher, and were buried forever. Then Christian said with a merry heart, "He has given me rest by His sorrow and life by His death."

Forgiveness is a miracle which God performs. I do not explain it. I simply say:

> In my hand no price I bring;
> Simply to Thy Cross I cling.

8

Forgive Yourself

I talked with a man who was in such a nervous state he could not do his work. His business was going down, his home life was unhappy, he was avoiding his friends, and had started drinking heavily.

We found that his trouble stemmed from a terrible thing he had done some years before. He had tried to forget it, but the thought of it was increasingly in his mind. He would think about it during the day and even dream about it at night. His mind had become almost completely obsessed by this one memory.

It was something that required no restitution, and now there was nothing he could do about it. But he was deeply repentant and seemed to me to meet every condition of forgiveness. I read and explained to him the Fifty-first Psalm. Then we got on our knees and prayed for God's forgiveness.

I feel absolutely sure that God completely forgave that man that day, that the Father wiped the slate clean and remembered the man's sin against him no more. I told him that and he believed it. I felt he would be all right.

But the next week he came back, no better than he had been. I said to him, "God has done something for you that you are unwilling to do for yourself. You asked God to forgive you, and He did, but you have not forgiven yourself." He agreed, but insisted he could not get it out of his mind.

I reminded him that in the New Testament Jesus tells us

to become as little children. I asked him if he remembered ever falling down and hurting himself when he was a little boy. Of course, he remembered.

"When that happened," I asked, "what did you do?" He did what all of us have done. He went crying to his mother and she would kiss the bruised places and, in some mysterious manner, the pain would go away and he would feel well again. He smiled as he thought about it.

Then I suggested that now he be like that little boy. I told him that he had bruised his heart, his soul, his conscience, that it hurt terribly, but that the great Father would kiss the pain away if only he would believe. I told him to believe in God just as he used to believe in his mother. Not to be big and important, but to have the simple faith of a little boy.

Again we knelt together, and I prayed, "Father, here is one of Thy children who is hurt. Now he has come to You as he used to go to his mother. He is kneeling at Your knee. Take his pain away—right now." We got up, and he said, "For the first time I feel it is gone." And I can report that today, after some months, he is a radiant, happy man.

There are many people who are living a condemned life because they never learned to accept the forgiveness of God, that is, to forgive themselves. Many people carry on their minds an accumulation of past mistakes, failures, and sins. It becomes a burden that no person can bear. It produces terrific mental strain, nervousness, fear, and worry.

Walt Whitman said: "I think I could turn and live with animals, they are so placid and self-contained. . . . They do not lie awake in the dark and weep for their sins." It is true that animals do not feel guilt. But it is also true that animals do not write poetry, as did Walt Whitman.

In man there is something good and fine. He is made so that he can "lie awake and weep over his sins." Take that out of man and he would be no more than an animal. But a sense of guilt can turn a strong man into an invalid. It can produce all sorts of functional disorders. It can wreck one's mind.

One can be so overwhelmed with a sense of guilt that one of three things happens. He will be turned into an animal without conscience or hope. Or life will become unbearable, as it did for Judas. Or one will accept and be loosed by an experience of forgiveness—God's forgiveness, and then his own.

Time and again I have read to myself and to others a poem that Ernest Rogers wrote, which he called "Another Chance." One of the verses goes:

> But down on my trembling knees I fall,
> Though others may look askance,
> To say a prayer to the Lord of All,
> The God of another chance.

No matter what you have done, remember, "If my people, which are called by my name, shall humble themselves, and pray, and seek my face, and turn from their wicked ways; then will I hear from heaven, and will forgive their sin, and will heal their land" (2 Chronicles 7:14).

9
Unanswered Prayers

Prayer is the subject of more letters that come to me than any other subject. Many people write requests for prayer, many ask how they should pray in regard to a particular situation, many ask why they have not had an answer to some specific prayer. Often someone writes, "The Bible says, 'Ask, and it shall be given you.' I have asked but it has not been given me."

Many whose prayers are not answered are bitter and resentful. They wonder if God plays favorites and hears only certain ones. Many are confused and frustrated. They have prayed and now they do not know which way to turn.

In reply, I want to say, first, that God does hear and answer prayer. In "The Cotter's Saturday Night," Robert Burns said, "They never sought in vain that sought the Lord aright!" Underscore that word *aright*—that is the key. The Bible tells us, "Ye ask, and receive not, because ye ask amiss . . ." (James 4:3). As I read the Bible I find listed many causes of unanswered prayer. Look at some of the more common ones:

"And ye returned and wept before the Lord; but the Lord could not hearken to your voice, nor give ear unto you" (Deuteronomy 1:45). Through His servant Joshua, God had told the people what to do; they paid no attention and did as they pleased. God's later refusal to hear their prayers was the result of their disobedience. One condition of prayer is our willingness to obey God in our lives.

Jeremiah 29:13 tells us: "And ye shall seek me, and find me, when ye shall search for me with all your heart." Half-heartedness is another cause of unanswered prayer. If we are not entirely dedicated to our own prayers, we should not expect God to waste time with us.

The Bible tells us, "If I regard iniquity in my heart, the Lord will not hear me" (Psalms 66:18). That does not mean that one must be perfect in order to pray. Surely even the vilest can pray. It does mean that we must "abhor" evil; that the desire of our hearts is to live right.

"But let him ask in faith, nothing wavering. . . . A double minded man is unstable in all his ways" (James 1:6–8). Stability is required of one who would pray. Our minds and hearts must have a fixed purpose and we must hold steadfastly to that purpose.

By far, the main reason for unanswered prayers is that our prayers are not within the will of God. Our Lord was careful to add to His prayer, ". . . nevertheless not my will, but thine, be done" (Luke 22:42). We do not have full understanding; and even though one is completely sincere, from God's view it may be clearly seen that his prayer is not best. Our faith must be such that we trust Him with the answer. Let us ever be mindful that our larger prayer is that we be fully surrendered to God's will.

THREE ESSENTIALS FOR PRAYER

It has been beautifully said, "Between the humble and contrite heart and the majesty of heaven there are no barriers; the only password is prayer." It bothers me that so few people seem to use that "password" and thereby deny unto themselves so many of the blessings of heaven which are available to them.

"The humble and contrite heart" is the first essential. One of the finest verses in the Bible is 2 Chronicles 7:14: "If my people, which are called by my name, shall humble themselves, and pray. . . ." Notice that we are not told to pray for humility; we are told to humble ourselves. It is such a temptation to become proud, to feel self-sufficient, to recognize no need for God. Sometimes we must be put on our backs before we ever look up.

Too many of us are like the Pharisee in the Temple who prayed, "I thank thee, that I am not as other men are . . ." (Luke 18:11). We compare ourselves with someone who has failed along the way and we take secret pride in another's downfall. That is the reason we are so attracted to gossip—it makes us look so good in comparison! Not enough of us are like the publican who prayed, "God be merciful to me a sinner" (Luke 18:13).

Not only must one be humble in order to pray; he must also have faith. There is probably no passage in the Bible which I read more often than Mark 11:22–26; that is the passage which describes how faith can remove mountains, and in which Jesus said, "I say unto you, What things soever ye desire, when ye pray, believe that ye receive them, and ye shall have them."

Believing is a process of mental picturing. So often, instead of picturing the answer we want, we continue to look at the troubles we have. We concentrate on our fears instead of our faith, our problems instead of our powers, our sins instead of our Saviour.

In that same passage, after He had talked about faith and

believing, Jesus said something else: "And when ye stand praying, forgive, if ye have ought against any. . . ." A wrong spirit toward another person, hate, hurt feelings, envy, jealousy, can block our prayers completely out.

Humility and faith are two essentials of effective prayer. The third essential you will find in John 15:7: "If ye abide in me, and my words abide in you, ye shall ask what ye will, and it shall be done unto you." *Abide*—that is the key word. Sometimes the answer comes immediately, sometimes the answer tarries—but we must continue close to Christ, developing our love for Him, allowing His love to fill our own lives more completely, meditating day and night upon His words.

Jesus said, ". . . men ought always to pray, and not to faint" (Luke 18:1). "To faint" means "to give up, to quit." Many times we miss the answer because we stop praying too soon. *Humility, faith, abide*—those are the three key words to answered prayer.

A-C-T-S-S

It is easy to get into a spiritual rut and reach the place where we go through the motions without receiving the power. Especially is this true in our praying. It is a temptation to say the same words every time we pray, without really thinking and without putting our hearts into what we are saying. I am constantly seeking to develop new spiritual techniques.

Recently I have hit upon a word that I like to keep in mind when I pray. The word is ACTSS ("acts" with an extra *s*). It is an appropriate word for prayer because all prayer should result in acts. I needed that extra *s* because I use the word as an outline for prayer.

A is for adoration. Surely all prayer should begin with our thinking of the Lord. The most wonderful collection of prayers is the Psalms. Sometime read some of the Psalms, noting how much is given to praise of God: "O Lord our Lord, how excellent is thy name in all the earth!" (8:1); "I will sing unto the Lord, because he hath dealt bountifully with me" (13:6).

Kahlil Gibran, in *The Prophet*, says, "You pray in your distress and in your need; would that you might pray also in the fullness of your joy and in the days of abundance." All real prayer begins in adoration of God.

C is for confession. As one feels the presence of God, as one thinks of His purity and righteousness, he naturally feels even as Isaiah felt. When Isaiah saw the Lord high and lifted up, he fell on his face, saying, "I am undone; because I am a man of unclean lips . . ." (6:5). We read, "If we confess our sins, he is faithful and just to forgive us our sins, and to cleanse us from all unrighteousness" (1 John 1:9). That is a wonderful promise.

T is for thanksgiving. One of my favorite songs is, "Count your many blessings, name them one by one." Many people never think of God except when they want something. Like any father, God is glad when His children come asking; but don't you suppose He also wants us to talk with Him sometimes about so much that He has already given?

S is for supplication; that is, prayer for others. In 1 Samuel 12:23 we read, "God forbid that I should sin against the Lord in ceasing to pray for you. . . ." Notice the wording in the Lord's Prayer: the pronouns "our" and "us" predominate. Never forget—praying for another person makes a difference to that person.

The last *S* is for submission: ". . . not my will, but thine, be done" (Luke 22:42). Prayer is not a means by which I seek to control God; it is a means of putting myself in a position where God can control me. Instead of my prayer being "Give me," it must become "Make me."

10

Give Yourself Away

Jesus gave us one of the supreme principles of life when He said, "He that findeth his life shall lose it: and he that loseth his life . . . shall find it." These words are recorded in the tenth chapter of Matthew (v. 39), a chapter every Christian ought to study carefully.

In this chapter are the names of the twelve men Jesus chose to be His disciples, and His instructions to them. He told them of their mission in life and said that they were not to worry about providing for themselves. "Provide neither gold, nor silver, nor brass in your purses," He said (v. 9). He reminded them that they would meet opposition and would be persecuted, but they were not to fear "them which kill the body, but are not able to kill the soul . . ." (v. 28).

Jesus told His disciples that they could afford to trust their safety and security in the hands of their Father. He pointed out how God notes even the fall of one sparrow, and He said, "Fear ye not therefore, ye are of more value than many sparrows" (v. 31). He charged His disciples that the one thing they were to fear was that they might lose their courage and fail to confess their Lord. He said, ". . . whosoever shall deny me before men, him will I also deny before my Father which is in heaven" (v. 33).

Following Jesus means that He must be put first. He demands that love for Him must take precedence above even the love we have for our own families—our fathers or mothers, our sons or daughters; there can be no rivals to our affection for Him. "He that loveth father or mother more than me is not worthy of me: and he that loveth son or daughter more than me is not worthy of me" (v. 37).

It is very popular today to say that religion can make one successful, happy, confident, and relaxed. But Jesus doesn't appeal to the selfish desires of those who would follow Him. Instead, following Him demands a cross. His words were: ". . . he that taketh not his cross, and followeth after me, is not worthy of me" (v. 38).

There is a little book entitled *The Cross in Christian Experience,* written by Dr. W. M. Clow. In that book Dr. Clow distinguishes between a burden, a thorn, and a cross; no one I know has been able to say it better. He says that a burden is the normal load which life lays upon every man—his daily work and responsibilities. A thorn is an affliction which some must bear—it may be a handicap, an illness, a deep sorrow, or one of many things. The cross is a voluntary denial of ourselves in order to carry His load. Burdens and thorns are thrust upon us, but only volunteers carry crosses.

DON'T BE A HOLD-OUT

Then Jesus comes to the supreme law of discipleship and of life. Give yourself away, He says; don't be a hold-out. Be willing to lose yourself and your life for His sake, and He promises that you will find life anew. I heard it said of a young man recently, "He has not found himself." Many people are in that predicament!

Some years ago a tailor phoned to say that a man had bought me a suit. When I went down to get measured and to select the cloth, the tailor said, "The man wants you to have the best," and he showed me the most expensive cloth he had. A couple of weeks later the suit was delivered to me.

It fit me perfectly. It was the finest suit I had ever had. Never have I been prouder of a suit. But it was so nice that I wanted to wear it only on special occasions. When I went away I never took that suit because I thought it might get worn. I didn't want to put it in my bag because it might get wrinkled. In fact, there were very few occasions when I wanted to wear my good suit, and through nearly ten years I kept it.

One day that same tailor was measuring me for another suit. I said, "You remember that first suit you made for me? I still have it." He said, "Why you can't wear that suit. It is out of style." Not only was it out of style; from hanging in my closet so long, it had actually become badly worn. By holding it out, I had lost my good suit. I had saved it to death.

Down in Mississippi I had dinner in the home of an elderly lady. Her children were grown up and gone; her husband had died; now she was alone. During dinner I commented on the lovely tablecloth. After dinner she opened a large chest and carefully lifted out some of the most exquisite linens I have ever seen.

She told me that when she was a young lady, her mother had taught her to sew and had helped to make these lovely things. When she married she had her chest filled—I think that is what they call a "hope chest." I asked, "When do you use these lovely things?" Rather sadly she replied, "I never have used them." Now it is too late; the one she made them for is gone. She actually lost her lovely things by saving them.

When I first began preaching, I had difficulty getting up enough to say. I spoke of this to my father who had been preaching a long time. During our conversation, I told him of a very fine illustration I had read. He said, "Why don't you use that in your sermon next Sunday?" I replied, "I am saving that for a special occasion." Then my father gave me the best lesson I ever received in the art of preaching. He said, "Use everything you have in your next sermon; then you will find something else."

I have a minister-friend who has the finest filing system I have ever seen. But the tragedy is that he has spent so much time saving his material that he has never had time to prepare his sermons. The result is that he has pretty much lost out as a preacher.

Saving is a virtue that may become a fault.

ALL THE WAY

One of our favorite hymns has these words:

> Where He leads me, I will follow,
> I'll go with Him, with Him all the way.
>
> E. W. BLANDY

The truth is, you can't go with Him at all unless you decide to go "all the way." In fact, that principle applies in so many areas of life.

A young man who is near and dear to me recently went to another city to begin a new job. He wanted to make good, and we talked about it. I told him not to worry about how much he was paid or how soon he got a raise. I told him not to worry about his position; if he were told to sweep the floor, he should sweep it the best it has ever been swept. I told him to forget his own pleasures and give himself to his work. I know that if he follows that path, he will find the life he really wants.

When my wife and I got married she had one hundred

dollars that she had saved up from her salary as a schoolteacher. She gave it to me to put in the bank with my money. Actually I didn't have any money in the bank, but I hadn't told her because I was afraid she wouldn't marry me if she knew how poor I was. I told her that the money was hers and she should keep it for special things that she might want. She said, "No, I don't want anything that isn't ours." That is really the only way a marriage can work. You must put all you have into it.

We could all be happier and accomplish so much more if we weren't afraid to turn loose and give our best. I got a letter from a lady who said that for some years she had wanted to tithe, but she didn't have the courage. Finally she did take the plunge and started giving a tenth of her income. She told me what a great joy it has brought to her life.

You remember when your children were little. You could stand one on a high place, hold out your arms, and tell him to jump to you. The child would leap forward into space. Of course, you could have jumped back and let the child fall and get hurt. But the child never thought about your doing such a thing. He had faith in you and knew that your arms would catch him and hold him.

Our Lord wants us to have that sort of faith in Him. So before He said, ". . . he that loseth his life for my sake . . ." (Matthew 10:39), He told us that God notes the fall of even one little sparrow, and He said, "Fear ye not therefore, ye are of more value than many sparrows" (Matthew 10:31). The Psalmist said, "I have been young, and now am old; yet have I not seen the righteous forsaken, nor his seed begging bread" (37:25). Come to think of it, neither have I. Have you ever seen the righteous forsaken?

Where in your life have you been holding out from the

Lord? Is there some sin you should let go? Some cross you should lift up? Why not trust Him now and by faith lose your life for His sake. He promises that you will find the very life you have been holding back.

PART II

HOPE

11

Learn to Hope

One morning I ran across this saying: "Life is full of glad surprises for those who hope." It stuck in my mind, and I found myself repeating it over and over. At noon that day I spoke to a group of businessmen and, as I often do, I spoke too long, making me late for another appointment.

I rushed out to catch a bus back to my study, but just as I got to the stop, the bus pulled off, and I missed it. I was about to get fretted when I thought of the saying, "Life is full of glad surprises for those who hope."

So, instead of fretting, I stood there on the corner, hoping. In less than two minutes a man stopped in a big Cadillac and offered me a ride.

On our way, we talked about several things, then he said to me, "You are doing a lot of things, and you need a rest." I had heard that before, however, so paid no attention.

But then he said, "I own a lovely hotel down in Daytona, Florida, and I want you and your family to go down there and stay as long as you can." Then he said the most important thing, "You will be my guests, absolutely without charge."

After I got out of his car, having graciously accepted his invitation, I just stood there thinking about it. So often we foolishly fix our minds on things we have missed in life when, instead, we ought to be looking ahead and hoping for something better to come along.

Dr. Samuel Johnson, one of the greatest minds England ever produced, once declared that to have a bright outlook on life was worth a thousand pounds a year. It pays off, even financially, to think optimistically.

When I got back to my study that day, I read again Psalms 42:5: "Why art thou cast down, O my soul? and why art thou disquieted in me? hope thou in God: for I shall yet praise him for the help of his countenance."

"Hope thou in God." That is to say, when you are discouraged and disquieted, put God in the center of your thinking. Plant deep in your mind the persistent, persuasive feeling that God is on your side, and, somehow, everything will be all right.

The Psalmist says that if you will do that, there will come a time when you will have reason for praise because of what God did for you.

One of the greatest men who ever walked this earth was Abraham. In explaining his greatness, Saint Paul says in Romans 4:18, "Abraham, who against hope believed in hope." Moffatt's translation makes that clearer: "For Abraham, when hope was gone, hoped on in faith." There were times when things looked very dark for Abraham. He went out "not knowing whither he was going." But no matter what happened, he kept on hoping—looking and working for something better. And that something better did come.

I have before me a letter from a friend telling me of a marvelous change that has come into his life. He says, "I have something else to think about, and a new hope."

Certainly it is true that "life is full of glad surprises for those who hope."

Hope deferred maketh the heart sick.

Proverbs 13:12

12
Hope Deferred

Look through the eyes of John's Gospel at those people gathered about the pool at Bethesda. It is a wretched sight. There "lay a great multitude of impotent folk, of blind, halt, withered . . ." (John 5:3). It was the gathering place for those of that city who were crippled, sick, blind, helpless, and friendless. It comes as no surprise to read that Jesus was there, also. He seemed to always be where there was someone in need.

These people were not without hope. They believed that an angel came at certain times and troubled the water. The first one to step into the pool after the troubling of the water would be healed. Jesus fixed His eyes on one man who had been there for thirty-eight years. What a marvelous hope that man had! The Bible tells us that "Hope deferred maketh the heart sick." Imagine a hope that can live for thirty-eight years! Some people lose hope at their very first disappointment.

Deferred hope is truly no respector of persons. In the very community in which each of us lives, there are numerous people to gather about our own town's Bethesda pool. There are those who live in the "lower end" of the city—the winos, alcoholics, dope addicts, prostitutes, and the disinherited.

Many of these are too sick to hope any longer.

Just a little way up the street we find the economically poor, the racial minorities, and the uneducated. Many are still hoping that a busy, affluent society will accord them the privilege of being accepted as human beings.

Go into every section of the town and there are people sickened by deferred hope. Many have learned that one can be lonely in a crowd. They have learned that loneliness is different from aloneness or solitude. Loneliness is the feeling of being left out from others. How many are there who have turned away from an empty mailbox after the postman has gone by, or sat by a phone waiting for it to ring, or listened for a knock on the door that is delayed day after day after day?

Hope deferred—there are those who are sick, hoping for a cure to be discovered. Others have kept hoping for word about a loved one lost in action in some war. The list of those holding hopes which are deferred is endless. In fact, in many the hope has faded out and in its place has come to live despair, or disappointment, or bitterness, or any other member of the family of hopelessness. Hope can die.

But we had hoped that he was the one to redeem Israel.
Luke 24:21 RSV

13

Broken Dreams

On the afternoon of the day of our Lord's Resurrection, He saw two sad people walking along the road from Jerusalem to Emmaus. Unrecognized, Jesus fell in step with them and they talked as they went along together. Thinking their traveling companion was a stranger who did not know what had happened, they explained who Jesus was and how He had been crucified.

Then they said with sorrow, "But we had hoped that he was the one to redeem Israel." We note that their hope is past tense. Here is hope that is dead—"We had hoped."

God gave man the capacity to hope—to dream—to see beyond what is to what might be.

For man is dreaming ever,
  He glimpses the hills afar,
And plans for the things out yonder
  Where all his tomorrows are:
And back of the sound of the hammer,
  And back of the hissing steam,
And back of the hand on the throttle,
  Is ever a daring dream.

AUTHOR UNKNOWN

But sometimes dreams do not become reality. The great and beloved preacher, Dr. J. Wallace Hamilton, has a chapter entitled "Shattered Dreams" in his book *Horns and Halos in Human Nature.* He tells of the weirdest auction sale in history. It was held in the city of Washington in 1926. One hundred fifty thousand patent models of old inventions were declared obsolete and put up for sale. The people would laugh as things were put up, such as a bedbug buster and an illuminated cat to scare away mice. There was a gadget that enabled a mother to churn the milk and rock the baby in one operation. There was a device to prevent snoring, which consisted of a trumpet reaching from the mouth to the ear. It was designed to awaken the snorer instead of the neighbors. One man invented a tube to reach from his mouth to his feet so his breath would keep his feet warm while he slept. There was an adjustable pulpit which could be raised or lowered. The auctioneer told how a preacher in Ohio was preaching on the subject "Where Will You Spend Eternity?" During his sermon he accidentally hit the button on the pulpit, and down he went.

That auction of old patent models was good for 150,000 laughs. But look deeper and we see it also represented 150,000 broken dreams. Somebody had high hopes for each of those inventions. Long hours of work were put into each one of them. Many hoped for fame and fortune to result. Some died in poverty, trying to sell what they had invented. One hundred fifty thousand dead hopes!

In His most beloved story, Jesus told of the young man who "gathered all together, and took his journey into a far country . . ." (Luke 15:13). He envisioned an exciting and good life, a time of freedom and joy. In some form or another, this dream has possessed the minds of great numbers of people. Many believe that out yonder somewhere, away from the restraint of day, is true happiness. It is a high hope which sends many out. The prodigal son ended up at a hog trough. His hopes were shattered.

There among the hogs he seized upon a new hope. "How many hired servants of my father's have bread enough and to spare . . . I will arise and go to my father . . ." (Luke 15:17, 18). Hope died, but a new hope was born.

A good example of how one can start again after seemingly total defeat comes out of the life of Thomas Carlyle. There was a period in his life when he was living in almost total poverty and defeat. During this time he labored to write the first volume of the history of the French Revolution. It was his greatest work, and he felt it would bring to him the literary success he sought. When he had finally completed the first volume, he took it to John Stuart Mill to read. Mill sat by his fire and carefully read the remarkable work page by page. One morning his maid was cleaning the room and, seeing the disarrayed pages of the manuscript on the floor by Mill's chair, she thought they were papers he had discarded, so she used them to build a fire.

When Carlyle learned that the work into which he had put so much was destroyed, he was a depressed and defeated man. He had neither the strength nor the heart to start over. He vowed he would never write again. For days and days he brooded over his misfortune. Then one day he looked out the window and saw a man building a brick wall. He watched as the man picked up one brick at a time and set it in place.

As Carlyle watched, he decided he would write his book again, by writing one page at a time. So it was that the hope which had died began to live again.

I hope to see you in passing as I go to Spain.

Romans 15:24 RSV

14

Failure Turned to Blessing

Saint Paul was writing to the Romans. He told them that he hoped to see them on his way to Spain. Going to Spain was his great dream, his high hope. But Paul never got to Spain. Instead, a prison cell in Rome was where his journey ended. It has been well said that every man dreams of one life and is forced to live another. Many "die with all their music in them," as Oliver Wendell Holmes said, but many learn to sing again. Out of frustrations, disappointments, and dead hopes can come new life. One of the lessons we learn as we read biographies is that very few get to live life on the basis of his or her first choice. Most persons have to settle for a second or third choice.

Some years ago I went to Enterprise, Alabama, to speak. In the center of the town I saw the strangest monument I have ever seen. It is a goddess on a lighted pedestal, holding aloft a giant boll weevil. As we all know, the boll weevil is the deadly enemy of cotton. This insect swept across the South and impoverished the farmers. My first thought was that these people had put on that pedestal their great enemy to remind themselves to keep on hating him. But not so. On the base of the monument is this inscription: In profound appreciation of the boll weevil, and what it has done as the herald of prosperity, this monument was erected by the citizens of Enterprise, Coffee County, Alabama.

I inquired and learned the story. In the year 1919, the boll weevil came and destroyed the cotton crops. The area was dependent on cotton, and this was a great calamity. At that time the people had almost no way to fight the new enemy. They seemed to be facing a hopeless situation. But somebody tried planting peanuts, and it was discovered that the climate and soil in that area were ideally suited for peanuts. This area became the peanut-growing capital of the world, and the people became more prosperous than they had ever been. Out of a tragedy a new hope came.

The story comes to mind of that night when the disciples of Jesus were caught in a storm at sea. The waves beat over the sides of the ship until it was almost filled with water. It appeared that sinking was imminent. They had done their best, but they could not cope with the storm. Many people have had this very experience. They have been overcome by circumstances beyond their control. There come times when it is hard to keep on hoping.

Jesus was asleep in the stern of the ship. The disciples woke Him up and said, "Master, carest thou not that we perish?" (Mark 4:38). They were not the last ones to wonder if God cares. Sometimes in seeming hopelessness we can believe that we are forgotten, even by God. But Jesus rose and said, "Peace, be still" (v. 39). The wind ceased and the sea became calm. Then He said to the disciples, "Why are ye so fearful? how is it that ye have no faith?" (v. 40). The disciples said to each other, "What manner of man is this, that even the wind and the sea obey him?" (v. 41). Out of a seemingly hopeless situation they gained a new faith.

I have often remembered a sentence from Lloyd C. Douglas's book *White Banners*—"sometimes a disappointment closes a door in a person's face, and then he looks about for some other door, and opens it, and gets something better than he had been hunting for the first time."

Not every failure turns into blessing. Not every sorrow brings out the sunshine of life. Not every prison opens into glorious service. Some people are forced to live out the balance of their years with a broken body, a broken home, a broken heart. But listen to the testimony of Saint Paul:

> . . . five times received I forty stripes save one. Thrice was I beaten with rods, once was I stoned, thrice I suffered shipwreck, a night and a day I have been in the deep. In journeying often, in perils of waters, in perils of robbers, in perils by mine own countrymen, in perils by the heathen, in perils in the city, in perils in the wilderness, in perils in the sea, in perils among false brethren; In weariness and painfulness, in watchings often, in hunger and thirst, in fastings often, in cold and nakedness.
>
> 2 Corinthians 11:24–27

What a list of hurting, disappointing, frightening experiences! But through his trials he carried a bright hope and was able to write to the Romans, as Dr. Moffatt beautifully translates it, "No one who believes in him . . . will ever be disappointed. . . . No one" (Romans 10:11 MOFFATT).

We are saved by hope.

Romans 8:24

15
Saved by Hope

Hanging in the Tate Gallery in London is George Frederic Watts's great painting entitled *Hope.* It pictures a blindfolded woman sitting on the world, stricken and dejected. In her hand is a harp with all the strings broken except one. She is striking that one string and her head is bent toward it in closest attention to catch its sound. This is the artist's picture of hope, triumphant over the world's sin and sorrow, triumphant over anything and everything that can hurt a human being. When all else is gone, one still has hope left and hope can triumph.

There are many stories of people who were inspired by Watts's painting. One that I like tells of a man who was on his way to drown himself. On the way he saw this painting in a store window. He looked carefully at the blindfolded woman on her world of misery, playing on the one string. Finally he said, "Well, I have one string—I have a little boy at home," and he retraced his steps.

In one form or another, that story can be repeated countless times. No matter how bad life is, if one will only look, he can always find one hope that is left and that one hope can be the saving power.

Life can weigh heavily on a person and can eventually

break one down. Another painting which comes to mind is Jean François Millet's *Man With Hoe.* Some believe the French artist intended to show the dignity of labor. Others see the painting as showing one who is weary, crushed, and defeated. Look at the painting and you see a man leaning upon his hoe. That hoe is the heaviest-looking hoe one can imagine.

Edwin Markham saw Millet's painting and was moved to write:

> Bowed by the weight of centuries he leans
> Upon his hoe and gazes on the ground,
> The emptiness of ages in his face,
> And on his back the burden of the world.

Add just one little letter of the alphabet to that phrase and instead of "Man with hoe," you get "Man with hope." What a difference it makes to change "hoe" to "hope." We certainly would not eliminate hoes from the world. The hoe represents labor, and labor is of God. Sometimes we feel that life would be wonderful if we could give up our jobs and live in ease and comfort. It is not so. Someone has quoted Michelangelo, the great Italian sculptor, as saying, "It is only well with me when I have a chisel in my hand."

We are glad that men do have hoes and that we have opportunity to use our hoes. Unemployment is always a haunting horror. A painting of a man *without* a hoe would be worse—much worse. But along with his hoe, man also needs a hope. There is an old slave song of protest and escape—

> Hang up the shovel and the hoe,
> Take down the fiddle and the bow.

This is not the answer. Every man needs his hoe—his work. The hoe is not a hopeless instrument. It is quite the contrary. The man in the field with his hoe is looking toward a harvest, a harvest that will feed and clothe him and his loved ones. The man with the hoe has a reward to look forward to. Hoe and hope go hand in hand. It is when the man loses his hope that he "leans upon his hoe and gazes on the ground." Hoes are not made for leaning on. A hoe is for hoeing and the hope of the harvest is what makes all the difference.

The world's salvation will not be found in some great hoe-dropping movement. No one ever finds life's greatest happiness through escape.

Andrew Carnegie was fond of saying, "Three generations from shirtsleeves to shirtsleeves." What this means is that children of rich men have a hard time finding the moral equivalent of the struggles through which their fathers obtained their wealth. Man is not born to be satisfied. When man is satisfied he becomes bored, and boredom leads to self-destruction. We are made strong by the struggle. Look at the lives of the early pioneers, who faced harsh climates, sparse land, and endless toil. Out of their efforts came a sturdy civilization. The unfriendly environment could not defeat them because in them was the hope of that civilization they were building.

There was a man named Henry P. Crowell who had tuberculosis. In his day there was no cure for this dreaded disease, and he was making his way west to die. The slow train he was on stopped at a station where nearby was a grain mill with a FOR SALE sign on it. He got off the train, bought the mill, and set to work to get it going again. That was the beginning of Quaker Oats. He made a fortune, overcame his tuberculosis, and lived past the age of ninety.

Sir Thomas Buxton said a wonderful thing:

> The longer I live the more deeply I am convinced that that which makes the difference between one man and another—between the weak and the powerful, the great and insignificant, is energy—invisible determination—a purpose once formed and then death or victory. This quality will do anything that has to be done in the world; and no talents, no circumstances, no opportunities will make one a man without it.

Underscore that phrase—"a purpose once formed and then death or victory." That breeds hope that saves.

Saint Paul based his declaration "We are saved by hope" (Romans 8:24) on two great truths. He started with a conviction that we are sons of God. He said, "For as many as are led by the Spirit of God, they are the sons of God" (Romans 8:14). Study man and you see he does not aimlessly drift through life. Man is a creature that is led. He has incentives that are beyond his physical self. Man is both physical and spiritual. If one lives just in the physical, is guided and controlled just by physical appetites and desires, he has none of life's great inspirations and incentives. If man is willing to be led by the Spirit of God, then he receives vision far beyond the mere physical. His spirit becomes stronger than his body and therein he finds power and salvation.

Then, following his declaration that we are saved by hope, Saint Paul affirms, "And we know that all things work together for good to them that love God, to them who are the called according to his purpose" (Romans 8:28). Here is a firm basis for hope. He does not say everything that happens is good. A lot of things that happen are not good. He believes that if man will consider all the experiences of his life, both the good and the bad, and cement them together with his love for God, then the sum total of his life will be good. That is, no matter what happens, keep on loving God and life will work out well. That is the basis of the hope that saves.

. . . but we glory in tribulations also: knowing that tribulation worketh patience; And patience, experience; and experience, hope.

Romans 5:3, 4

16
Facing Tribulation

Tribulation—patience—experience—hope. That is the order in which it comes. If man never had trouble, he would never have any hope. Troubles develop patience, which enables man to bear life as he goes on living. And as man lives he gains experience. As a result of experience in living, man can and does see reason for hope. If we could not look back and see victories gained over adverse circumstances, we would have no hope in the midst of the troubles we are experiencing today, or fear that we might experience tomorrow.

"It is history that teaches us to hope," said Robert E. Lee. That is absolutely true, whether we are seeing history as related to the world and all people or whether we are looking at history just in reference to our own lives. Memory is a great producer of hope.

Dr. Norman Vincent Peale has proclaimed the message of hope to numberless multitudes of people. He is one of my finest inspirations and one of the ministers to whom I personally owe the most. In 1960 he preached a sermon entitled "Why We Say Merry Christmas." In that sermon he told about an article by Arthur Gordon which appeared in *Reader's Digest.* Arthur Gordon experienced a dry period in his writing. His thoughts did not flow as they once had; he found difficulty in saying what he wanted to say. He felt neither inspiration nor creative ability. After struggling for a period of time, he consulted a loved family physician who was wise and mature.

After hearing Arthur Gordon's story, the doctor said, "Life has gone out of you? Is that so?" And he asked him, "When you were a child what did you like to do most? What gave you the greatest joy?"

Gordon replied that he had enjoyed going to the beach and listening to the waves and the sea gulls.

"All right," said the doctor, "you spend the whole day tomorrow at the beach—alone. Get there at nine in the morning and stay until six at night. Take no writing materials, no books or other reading materials, no radio.

"Now," he continued, "I am going to give you four prescriptions." He took four pages off his pad, wrote something on each of them, numbered them, and said, "Take this one at nine o'clock, number two at twelve o'clock, number three at three o'clock, and number four at six o'clock."

The next day Arthur Gordon went to the beach. He sat for a moment in his car feeling futile and foolish. Then he read prescription number one: "Listen intently." He got out of his car and walked up and down the beach for three hours, listening to the sounds that were there—the wind, the sea, the gulls.

After three hours of intent listening he took out the second prescription: "Try reaching back." He sat down between two sand dunes and tried reaching back in his memory, remembering happy experiences and high points of his life.

After three hours of remembering, he opened the third prescription which said, "Reexamine your motives." He asked himself why he wanted to write—to see his name in print? To make a lot of money? Or did he write because he wanted to help people? For three hours he reexamined his motives.

Then at six o'clock he turned to the fourth prescription which was, "Write your worries in the sand." He took a stick and wrote his worries. He walked away, but he looked back and saw the tide come in and wash away what he had written. He felt clean and renewed.

In the year 1860, Elizabeth Akers Allen, writing under the pen name of Florence Percy, sent a poem entitled "Rock Me to Sleep" to the *Saturday Evening Post,* in which she expressed this longing to remember. Her words have been caught up by many, many people in the years since. She said:

> Backward, turn backward, O Time, in your flight,
> Make me a child again, just for to-night!

Through the process of memory we can become children again and it can be an experience which can re-create hope.

One of my best friends is an official of a large company. He had developed a drinking problem and, with that, other problems had come. He had about reached the point of despair and hopelessness. He decided to take some days off. He drove a hundred miles to a rural community where his aged mother still lived at his old home. He slept in the bed where he had slept as a boy. He ate, at the kitchen table, the meals his mother fixed, just like he used to do. He took long walks in the field where he used to work as a farm boy.

Gradually his thoughts became the thoughts that had

possessed him as a youth. He thought of the big world and how he wanted to be a part of it. He dreamed, like he used to, of becoming a man people would respect and who would make a contribution to the world. He began to believe in himself again. He remembered his early ambitions. He kept telling himself how he once walked away from those fields and accomplished his dreams and that now he could do it again. He captured a new hope and a new life.

My father used to preach a sermon on the text "And Peter remembered . . ." (Luke 22:61). The title of his sermon was "The Memory That Saves."

Not long ago I went to preach again in one of the little churches where I started my ministry. It is located back in the mountains. The paved road ended at a sawmill about three miles from the church. Many cold winter mornings I parked my car at that sawmill and walked over the ice-covered dirt road to the church. The day I was back visiting, I stopped again at that sawmill and let my mind go back. As I sat there I kept asking myself the question "Why was I willing to walk through the cold snow and ice to that little church?" Not because of what they paid me, because in those Depression years they paid me almost nothing. Not because of the crowds of people who would be there, because there were never more than a dozen or so who came. Not because of any recognition I would receive. I kept remembering why I did go. That memory encourages and strengthens me now.

"Tribulation—patience—experience—hope." Not only in reference to our own personal experiences, but also when we think of the lessons of history, this formula works. It is a discouraging experience to look at all the problems and troubles of the world. "But no man who is correctly informed as to the past," said Thomas Macaulay, "will be disposed to take a morose or desponding view of the present."

As we study history we learn that the pathway of mankind has not been easy. There have been dark periods of war and economic depression. There have been storms and earthquakes and major catastrophes of all kinds. Diseases and hunger have sent so many to early graves. But in spite of everything that has happened, the record of mankind is one of progress. Out of each setback has come a new beginning and a powerful forward surge.

In times of crises there is a tendency to lose hope for the future. There are always those who are preaching the end of civilization. History teaches us that the world is not doomed, that there is still progress to be made and we are challenged by the promise of a better world ahead. John Greenleaf Whittier looked at history and was inspired to write:

> And, step by step, since time began,
> I see the steady gain of man.

In a message to Congress in 1941, Franklin D. Roosevelt looked toward a future which would be secured by four essential freedoms. The freedom of speech and expression is the first. The second is the freedom of every person to worship God in his own way. The third is freedom from want, and the fourth is freedom from fear. The proclamation of those four freedoms gave new hope to people who had just come through the agonies of the most destructive war the world had ever known.

The writer of Ecclesiastes said a long time ago, "Say not, 'Why were the former days better than these?' For it is not from wisdom that you ask this" (7:10 RSV). As we go back in memory to our own experiences and as we look at mankind's life, we find our hopes strengthened for both today and tomorrow.

In 1968 the Dallas Cowboys football team lost the championship game to the Cleveland Browns. It was a bitterly disappointing defeat. Speaking about that game, Tom Landry made some wise observations. He said in *Sports Illustrated:*

> Anyhow, that game and the one we lost to the Browns in the same playoffs the next year brought us a great deal of criticism. It may sound funny, but those games also helped us develop character as a team. When you lose the way we did, you can either come back disorganized, or you can come back and win again. No team could come back as we did after our 1970 shutout loss to St. Louis if we hadn't had the experience we had against Cleveland those two years and the great disappointment of the ice game against Green Bay in 1967. You can't turn yourself around if you don't have a backlog of adversity. The Apostle Paul says suffering brings on endurance, endurance brings character and character brings hope. Once you develop character you tend to always hope things will work out. The guy with character continues to do the best he can, even against the odds, and keeps a bright outlook.

Endicott Peabody, the famous headmaster of Groton School, summed it all up when he said to remember that things in life will not always run smoothly. Sometimes we will be rising toward the heights—then all will seem to reverse itself and start downward. The great fact to remember is that the trend of civilization itself is forever upward; that a line drawn through the middle of the peaks and the valleys of the centuries always has an upward trend.

That fact—and it *is* fact—is always cause for hope.

That they might set their hope in God, and not forget the works of God, but keep his commandments.

Psalms 78:7

17

The Blessing of Memories

Here we have memory, hope, and effort included together. The Psalmist is saying that God gave deliverance to His people. The remembering of that deliverance gives hope for the present. That hope brings inspiration to live for God in the future.

Living in a city can be a discouraging experience because we are confronted with so many problems. There are sections where the housing is inadequate and the people are poor. There are streets where it is dangerous to walk because of crime. Many people in the city are sick. There are those who are friendless and lonely, others who are discouraged and frustrated. In a city there are murders, rapes, automobile wrecks, and fires. There is polluted air. Every day people are buried who are dear to someone's heart. There is deep sorrow in the hearts of many people in every city. At times one feels a sense of hopelessness.

Many times during a year I drive out to the airport of my city and get on a plane. As the plane gains altitude I look out the window and see the city stretched below. It is a beautiful sight, especially at night, when all the lights of the city are shining. From the airplane one gets a much more satisfying view of the city than when one is making his way through the narrow streets. Even though there are problems in the city, from the heights one sees the beauty and majesty of the city and is inspired by it.

So it is with life. Living in the present, one is constantly confronted with the trials and troubles of life. But when one looks back at life through memory, like seeing the city from an airplane, he sees life as a whole. The hard places are not as visible, the pain and suffering is quieted, and the entire panorama is beautiful and inspiring. It is good to sing the hymn:

> When upon life's billows you are tempest tossed,
> When you are discouraged, thinking all is lost,
> Count your many blessings, name them one by one,
> And it will surprise you what the Lord hath done.
>
> E. O. EXCELL

Forget not the works of God—remember. Memory and hope are very closely connected. We use the same faculties to look both backward and forward. If we look back and see the works of God, we will be inspired to look into the future and believe there are blessings ahead. We will be inspired to "keep his commandments" if we believe that faithfulness and service will not go unrewarded.

Saint Paul declares confidently, "The sufferings of this present time are not worthy to be compared with the glory which shall be revealed in us" (Romans 8:18). This is a marvelous hope, but how can he be so sure? He says, "We know that all things work together for good to them that love God . . ." (v. 28). This has been proven by his own experience and observation. He can look back at life and see that it has worked out well. He can see this because he is looking at the total experience of life instead of one incident or moment. Because he can get the distant view of life backward, he can also get the distant view of life forward. He sees glory ahead.

He Leadeth Me

In pastures green? Not always; sometimes He
Who knoweth best, in kindness leadeth me
In weary ways, where heavy shadows be—

Out of the sunshine warm and soft and bright,
Out of the sunshine into darkest night;
I oft would faint with sorrow and affright—

Only for this—I know He holds my hand,
So whether in the green or desert land,
I trust, although I may not understand.

And by still waters? No, not always so;
Ofttimes the heavy tempests round me blow,
And o'er my soul the waves and billows go.

But when the storms beat loudest, and I cry
Aloud for help, the Master standeth by,
And whispers to my soul, "Lo, it is I."

Above the tempest wild I hear Him say,
"Beyond this darkness lies the perfect day,
In every path of thine I lead the way."

So, whether on the hill-tops high and fair
I dwell, or in the sunless valleys where
The shadows lie—what matter? He is there.

And more than this; where'er the pathway lead
He gives to me no helpless, broken reed,
But His own hand, sufficient for my need.

So where He leads me I can safely go;
And in the blest hereafter I shall know
Why in His wisdom He hath led me so.

AUTHOR UNKNOWN

. . . hope thou in God.

Psalms 42:5

18
Hope Thou in God

This is the greatest statement on hope in the Bible. It sums it all up. One of the Ten Commandments is: "Thou shalt not take the name of the Lord thy God in vain . . ." (Exodus 20:7). Often that has been interpreted as meaning using God's name as profanity. But sometimes our swearwords are more stupid than sinful. The most profane word in the English language is the word *hopeless.* To proclaim hopelessness is to deny the presence and power of God.

Time after time man has expressed hopelessness. In 1801 Wilberforce said that he dared not marry because the future was too unsettled. In 1806 William Penn said, "There is scarcely anything around us but ruin and despair." In 1848 Lord Shaftsbury said, "Nothing can save the British Empire from shipwreck." In 1849 Benjamin Disraeli said, "In industry, commerce, and agriculture there is no hope." In 1852 the dying Duke of Wellington said, "I thank God that I shall be spared from seeing the consummation of ruin that is settling in around us." In 1914 Lord Grey said, "The lamps are going out all over Europe; we shall not see them lit again in our lifetime."

We read and hear such expressions as these over and over. There are many who see no brightness in the future. To them all the good is past. Almost twenty thousand people a year commit suicide in the United States. They have lost all hope.

The Psalmist asked, "Why art thou cast down, O my soul? and why art thou disquieted in me?" (Psalms 42:5). There are as many answers to that question as there are people. My own observation leads me to believe that the chief cause of discouragement and despair is loneliness.

In his play *Orpheus Descending,* Tennessee Williams has one of the characters say a gloomy thing: "We're all of us sentenced to solitary confinement inside our own skins for life! . . . we got to face it, we're under a life-long sentence to solitary confinement inside our own lonely skins for as long as we live on this earth!"

One of the characters in *The Cocktail Party* by T. S. Eliot says much the same thing:

> What is hell? Hell is oneself,
> Hell is alone. . . . There is nothing to escape from
> And nothing to escape to. One is always alone.

Or one could turn to another play which is entitled *When Ladies Meet,* written by Rachel Crothers. One of the characters says that he hasn't found anything, except to know that he hasn't got anything that really counts. Nobody belongs to him—nobody whose very existence depends on him. He is completely and absolutely alone.

As the minister of a church located in the center of Houston, I see daily the problems of people. Loneliness is the problem I see the most. There is the loneliness of those who are old and sick and often forgotten. There is the loneliness of one cut off from a loved one by death. There is the loneliness of a youth whose parents cannot communicate with him. There are many types of lonely people. Loneliness in a crowded city seems to be the worst. Loneliness is different from being alone. It is different from solitude. Loneliness is the feeling of being isolated from others.

When the Psalmist said to himself, "Why art thou cast down," it is very likely it was because of loneliness, because he then says, "hope thou in God." There is One who is always near and available. If one really believes in God, he never lacks strengthening companionship. Faith in and fellowship with God overcomes our feelings of hopelessness.

W. Albert Donaldson, in *You Can Hope Again,* tells about a party of tourists who went to Lick Observatory to view the heavens. As they looked through the great telescope, an astronomer said, "You will see a cluster of stars called Hercules, which is the finest in the northern sky. You can count six thousand or more stars. Each star is a sun, and each one you see is probably larger than our sun. Probably each sun has planets, and there are possibly moons around each planet, and there may be life, both plant and animal, on these planets."

After coming down from the observation chair, one of the visitors said, "Did you say all those stars are suns?"

"Yes."

"Did you say they are all larger than our sun?"

"Yes."

"Can you tell how large our sun is?"

"Well," said the astronomer, "if the sun were a hollow shell, you could pour over a million earths into it, and there would still be much space left."

The visitor was lost in contemplation for a brief minute, and then he said, "Well, then I guess it doesn't matter what happens to us in the coming election."

When we think of the greatness of God, it overcomes our

feelings of helplessness and defeat. We are not lonely. Sidney Lanier was striken with tuberculosis. He felt deserted and defeated. One day he sat looking at the marsh on the coast of Georgia. He was moved to write:

> As the marsh-hen secretly builds on the watery sod,
> Behold I will build me a nest in the greatness of God.

I have read over and over a passage written by Ernest Hemingway in "A Natural History of the Dead":

> When that persevering traveller, Mungo Park, was at one period of his course fainting in the vast wilderness of an African desert, naked and alone, considering his days as numbered and nothing appearing to remain for him to do but to lie down and die, a small moss-flower of extraordinary beauty caught his eye. "Though the whole plant," says he, "was no larger than one of my fingers, I could not contemplate the delicate confirmation of its roots, leaves and capsules without admiration. Can that Being who planted, watered and brought to perfection, in this obscure part of the world, a thing which appears of so small importance, look with unconcern upon the situation and suffering of creatures formed after his own image? Surely not. Reflections like these would not allow me to despair; I started up and, disregarding both hunger and fatigue, travelled forward, assured that relief was at hand; and I was not disappointed.

Jesus told us that God is a father. To some people there is no inspiration in thinking thus. Fathers can be cruel, disappointing, unloving. We have all heard stories of children's hearts being broken at Christmas because of some unworthy father. A family of children went to bed on Christmas Eve, excitedly anticipating their presents the next morning. The father had gone to town that day with the list of toys to buy. Late that night he came home drunk. He had spent all his money and had completely forgotten the children. Now all the shops were closed.

Eagerly the children got up on Christmas morning and ran to see the presents, but their stockings were empty. There was nothing. Tears of disappointment flowed down their cheeks. They had every reason to hope except for the fact that the one upon whom their hopes were based proved to be untrustworthy.

The Psalmist said, ". . . the judgments of the Lord are true and righteous altogether" (Psalms 19:9). Many of us have experienced moments when we may have doubted this. Many afternoons my wife and I have driven to the edge of our city and turned into a lovely cemetery. We wind our way through that cemetery and stop. We get out and stand by two tiny graves. They are the graves of two little grandsons of ours. With great joy did we anticipate the birth of each of them. How we looked forward to playing with and loving those little boys. I prayed with all the faith I had for them. I asked God to let them live. Instead we buried them. I know about hurt and disappointment.

I have also lived long enough to know that one cannot judge the character of God based on the tragedies of this life. Leslie D. Weatherhead wrote a little book entitled *The Will of God.* It explains it better than anything else I have ever read. He talks about the intentional will of God, the circumstantial will of God, and the ultimate will of God. Sometimes things happen which God does not intend. Sometime God allows things to happen under the circumstances. But ultimately God's will triumphs. We sing:

Not now, but in the coming years,
It may be in a better land,
We'll read the meaning of our tears,
And there, sometime, we'll understand.

MAXWELL N. CORNELIUS

Saint Paul said, "Now we see through a glass, darkly . . ." (1 Corinthians 13:12). We do not understand so many things and we hope that the things which happen which we think are the worst, someday we will realize were the best. I gain strength from these words: "Behold, the eye of the Lord is on those who fear him, on those who hope in his steadfast love" (Psalms 33:18 RSV). Sometimes we trust God "on account of." Other times we trust God "in spite of." We sing:

Come, ye disconsolate, where'er ye languish,
Come to the mercy seat, fervently kneel;
Here bring your wounded hearts, here tell your anguish;
Earth has no sorrows that heaven cannot heal.

THOMAS MOORE

If there were no God who ruled over this universe, if there were no heavenly Father who watched over mankind, then hope would be an illusion. With no God, the world would be like a ship with no one in command, drifting aimlessly on the sea. But through all of life there is a guiding hand. There is one everlasting reason for hope—"hope thou in God."

Some of man's suffering comes through ignorance. Many children died because of diphtheria; many have gone through life crippled because of polio. But we found preventatives for these and many other things that have hurt people. We have hope that we will find the cure for cancer and for so many other things that have brought despair.

This hope is what builds hospitals and supports vast research programs.

Men suffer because of the brutality of other men. Children are mistreated by brutal parents; minorities are trampled by bigots; killing and destruction are brought about by wars. The list could go on and on. But we still cling to the hope that men can learn to live together in love, and that hope causes those of goodwill to keep trying.

Wickedness is not hopeless. Jonathan Edwards's sermon "Sinners in the Hands of an Angry God" typifies the preaching and thinking of a lot of people—if one does wrong, to h--- with him. But Jesus came to call sinners to repentance (Matthew 9:13). There is hope for every sinner. Robert Burns, the beloved Scotch poet, wrote a poem to the devil in which he had the audacity to hope that even Satan might be converted. There is hope for the worst sinners among us. There is hope for you and for me—no matter what sins we have committed and no matter how guilty we now feel. That is why we build churches and keep on preaching the gospel.

I have hoped in thy word.

Psalms 119:74

19

God's Promises

On every page of the Bible there are words of God that give reason for hope. Sometimes when I feel a bit discouraged, I begin reading some of the promises of God, while remembering a little verse:

He has never broken
Any promise ever spoken.

In the promises of God I find inspiration and new hope. Here let me tell of half a dozen promises which lift me up. If space permitted, I could list hundreds more.

". . . Whosoever believeth in him should not perish, but have everlasting life" (John 3:16). That is the greatest promise of all. "Whosoever" includes me. This means that in spite of my own unworthiness, because I believe in Christ I am not doomed. I hope for eternity. I can face death without fear.

"If ye ask any thing in my name, I will do it" (John 14:14). That is almost too good to be true. Of course, I know that to ask in His name is serious business. It means I must be dedicated to His plans and purposes. But I am promised that if I am sincerely committed to Christ, I can pray and my prayer will be granted.

"In the world ye shall have tribulation: but be of good cheer; I have overcome the world" (John 16:33). Tribulations in this world are many—sickness, poverty, handicaps, disappointments, and on and on the list goes. But in the midst of tribulations I can be a cheerful person because of the assurance that our Lord overcomes all of these.

"Blessed is the man that walketh not in the counsel of the ungodly . . . he shall be like a tree planted by the rivers of water, that bringeth forth his fruit in his season; his leaf also shall not wither; and whatsoever he doeth shall prosper" (Psalms 1:1, 3). A sense of failure will sooner or later come to every person. We dream and work but sometimes we do not seem to accomplish very much. We begin to wonder if our lives are worthwhile and if the efforts we have made really amount to anything. But we have the promise that if we are faithful, our lives will be fruitful and we will not end up as failures.

"Lo, I am with you alway . . ." (Matthew 28:20). I like the story of the Chinese man whose name was Lo. He had become a Christian and was reading the New Testament for the first time. When he got to the last verse in Saint Matthew, he became very excited. He told a friend, "The Lord Jesus wrote this for me because He said, 'Lo, I am with you alway.' " And he was correct. The Lord was speaking to him and to each and every one of us.

"If ye have faith as a grain of mustard seed, ye shall say unto this mountain, Remove hence to yonder place; and it shall remove; and nothing shall be impossible unto you" (Matthew 17:20). A full-grown and complete faith is not required. A mustard seed is very small. If one has only a little faith, like the seed, it can grow and can overcome the mountain of any difficulty. This means that we need not be defeated.

There truly is hope in God's Word. Often I come in at night after some engagement and before going to bed, I sit down for awhile and read the newspaper or watch the news on television. Much of the news is bad. It tells of the troubles people have suffered that day. If one only fills his mind with the happenings of today, he will have a tendency toward despair. So it is very important to also read some of the eternal words of God in order to balance our thinking.

In hope of eternal life, which God, that cannot lie, promised before the world began.

Titus 1:2

20
Eternal Life

On every page of the Bible there is a word to assure man that life on this earth is not all there is to know.

"The righteous hath hope in his death" (Proverbs 14:32).

"Today shalt thou be with me in paradise" (Luke 23:43).

"I am the resurrection, and the life: he that believeth in me. . . . shall never die" (John 11:25, 26).

"For we know that if our earthly house of this tabernacle were dissolved, we have a building of God, an house not made with hands, eternal in the heavens" (2 Corinthians 5:1).

"If in this life only we have hope in Christ, we are of all men most miserable" (1 Corinthians 15:19).

"And God shall wipe away all tears from their eyes; and there shall be no more death . . ." (Revelation 21:4).

The hope of life beyond this life has given so very many the strength to bear great suffering and toil. The old Negro slave had very little to look forward to on this earth. But he could keep going because he had a firm hope which enabled him to sing such songs as:

I looked over Jordan, and what did I see,
Coming for to carry me home?
A band of angels a-comin' after me,
Coming for to carry me home.

There were those early pioneers in our land who battled the hardships of the frontier. The winters were cold, the work was hard, they had almost no defense against sickness. In those days people died at an early age. But they kept going and one of their inspirations was to go to some little frame church on the Lord's day and sing:

There's a land that is fairer than day,
And by faith we can see it afar;
For the Father waits over the way,
To prepare us a dwelling place there.

In the sweet by and by,
We shall meet on that beautiful shore.

S. F. BENNETT

Fanny Crosby was blind from the time she was a baby. She wrote many wonderful songs, but perhaps her best was the one written out of hope of eternal life. She sang:

But O, the joy when I shall wake
Within the palace of the King!

And I shall see Him face to face.

There are those who belittle the songs that look forward to the next life. They would like to take out of our songbooks such songs as "When the Roll Is Called Up Yonder," "On Jordan's Stormy Banks I Stand," "When They Ring Those Golden Bells," and others. There are those who say such songs are merely escapist—that these songs merely look forward to deliverance from the world and its troubles instead of facing responsibly the problems of the world. But such is not the case. The hope of life beyond this life is the inspiration to man to live nobly and sacrificially in this life. If life on this earth were all there were, many would question that it is worth the struggle. The assurance of life eternal gives strength and meaning and purpose to the sufferings and struggles of this life. Hope of eternity causes us to want to do our best in the here and now.

C. S. Lewis said it well in *Christian Behavior:*

> Hope is one of the Theological virtues. This means that a continual looking forward to the eternal world is not (as some modern people think) a form of escapism or wishful thinking, but one of the things a Christian is meant to do. It does not mean that we are to leave the present world as it is. If you read history you will find that the Christians who did most for the present world were just those who thought most of the next. The Apostles themselves, who set on foot the conversion of the Roman Empire, the great men who built up the Middle Ages, the English Evangelicals who abolished the Slave Trade, all left their mark on Earth, precisely because their minds were occupied with Heaven. It is since Christians have largely ceased to think of the other world that they have become so ineffective in this. Aim at Heaven and you will get earth "thrown in": aim at earth and you will get neither.

There is an eternal struggle between life and death, between hope and despair. For us who are Christians, this struggle is best symbolized in the Easter story. Christ's followers had watched Him die and had seen Him buried in a tomb sealed with a large stone. Their world had crashed. Now they were frightened, purposeless people. But not all of those who loved Him were entirely without hope. In Saint Mark's story we read one of the most inspiring verses in the whole Bible: "And very early in the morning, the first day of the week, they came unto the sepulchre at the rising of the sun" (Mark 16:2). They knew a heavy stone sealed that sepulchre, and they did ask who would roll away the stone, but in the act of coming and in asking that question they were expressing their hope. They had not surrendered. In their minds they believed that somehow the stone could be rolled away. These faithful women had not surrendered to defeat. They did not expect the Resurrection, but at least they could anoint His body.

Those people who possess hope are never seeking an easy way out. They are not the ones who run away from the problems of their lives and their world. They are the ones who keep on believing that solutions can be found, that stones can be rolled away.

We can look at our world and see many stones in the way. There are some who are mere head-shakers or hand-wringers. They talk about how bad everything is and they see ahead only doom and destruction. But the hopeful persons in this life see "the rising of the sun" and are up and about on some important mission.

Blessed be the God and Father of our Lord Jesus Christ, which according to his abundant mercy hath begotten us again unto a lively hope by the resurrection of Jesus Christ from the dead.

1 Peter 1:3

21
Resurrection Power

The Resurrection of Jesus Christ is God's mightiest act. This is what literally created the Christian faith and is the ground of Christian hope. The noun *hope* does not appear in the four Gospels. Nowhere is Jesus quoted as using the word *hope.* For those who wrote the Gospels, hope was born with the Resurrection. Saint Paul and the other New Testament writers use the word hope often. Christ is alive, and on that fact Christian hope is founded.

The Resurrection of Christ means far more than the mere resuscitation of a dead body. There are numerous stories of bodies which have been brought back to life. We remember that Elisha revived the dead son of a widow from Shunem (2 Kings 4:32–37). Jesus raised the dead daughter of Jairus (Mark 5:21–43). Also, Jesus brought back to life the son of the widow from Nain (Luke 7:11–16). Lazarus lay four days in the tomb before Jesus raised him back to life (John 11:17). We have read more than one newspaper story of a dead body coming back to life. This is not the main point of the Resurrcction. In fact, Saint Paul never mentions the empty tomb.

The Resurrection of Christ was God's final designation of Him as His own Son. Saint Paul says, "... Jesus Christ ... declared to be the Son of God with power ... by the resurrection from the dead" (Romans 1:3, 4). Also, Saint Paul speaks of "the power of his resurrection" (Philippians 3:10). That means that through Christ a life can be transformed, can be saved now and forever. This is man's greatest hope. It means that man has hope both in this life and in the life to come.

Eternal life assures us of more than the mere survival of our souls. It means more than the continuation of life as we now know it. It affirms the fact that God will bring to completion His purposes for each of His children. Death cannot defeat God's plan for any one of us.

Certainly Christ gives hope to every one of us for this life. Let me quote here a poem that beautifully expresses our earthly hopes in Him:

The Miracle Dreams

That night when in Judean skies
  The mystic star dispensed her light,
A blind man moved amid his sleep,
  And dreamed that he had sight.

That night when shepherds heard the song
  Of hosts angelic choiring near,
A deaf man stirred in slumber's spell
  And dreamed that he could hear.

That night when in the cattle stall
  Slept child and mother cheek by jowl,
A cripple turned his twisted limbs,
  And dreamed that he was whole.

That night when o'er the new-born babe
The tender Mary rose to lean,
A loathsome leper smiled in sleep,
And dreamed that he was clean.

That night when to the mother's breast
The little King was held secure,
A harlot slept a happy sleep,
And dreamed that she was pure.

That night when in a manger lay
The Sanctified who came to save,
A man moved in the sleep of death,
And dreamed there was no grave.

SUSIE M. BEST

Not only "that night," but every night since He came, people have dreamed with new hope. Christ did not need to talk about hope. He was and He is the hope of every person and of the world. We rightly sing:

My hope is built on nothing less
Than Jesus' blood and righteousness.

EDWARD MOTE

Christ is our hope not only in this life, but beyond this life. "If in this life only we have hope in Christ, we are of all men most miserable," said Saint Paul (1 Corinthians 15:19).

Thy kingdom come. Thy will be done in earth, as it is in heaven.

Matthew 6:9

22
Prisoners of Hope

What a glorious hope that prayer of our Lord expresses for our world! There are those who can only see the world getting worse and worse. On every side we hear predictions of doom and destruction. We do not blind our eyes to the ills and wrongs of our society. There is so much in our world that is wrong. But neither do we surrender in defeat. If we can only believe that this creation is going to be abolished, then we must conclude that Christianity has nothing to offer man in his present predicament.

In the Book of Zechariah we read a thrilling challenge: "Return to your stronghold, O prisoners of hope . . ." (9:12 RSV). This was written during dismal, disappointing times. The holy city lay in ruin. The temple was destroyed. The people had been conquered and were downcast and afraid. Their voices were reduced to mere whispers or to silence. But the prophet shouts a clarion call: "Return to your stronghold." He tells them that they are not prisoners of defeat, or of helplessness, or of evil conquerors. He declares they are "prisoners of hope."

Being conquered and bound by hope, they are compelled to rise and face, in the language of Paul, their "heavenly vision." They are called to courage instead of fear, to sacrifice instead of surrender, to action instead of silence. Being "prisoners of hope," they cannot look at their world, as bad as it is, with hopelessness.

Truly, every Christian is, as Paul said of himself, "the prisoner of Jesus Christ" (Ephesians 3:1). Because He is the hope of the world, it therefore must follow that Christ's prisoners are "prisoners of hope." Christians believe that God cares about His world and is working with men to bring His kingdom on earth. At times progress seems mighty slow and it seems some of the time that wrong is on the throne. But we who are bound by hope must always believe:

And behind the dim unknown,
Standeth God within the shadow,
Keeping watch above his own.

JAMES RUSSELL LOWELL

This hope compels us to keep working at our task of giving all we have in Christ's service. "God so loved the world, that he gave his only begotten son . . ." (John 3:16). Jesus came bringing a message of peace, righteousness, and love. He gave to the world a hope that is both beautiful and transforming. We cannot believe that God will allow His Son's mission to fail. Because of our hope, we sing, "The Kingdom Is Coming," and we give ourselves to that end.

I live for those who love me,
For those who know me true,
For the heaven that smiles above me,
And awaits my spirit too;
For the cause that lacks assistance,
For the wrong that needs resistance,
For the future in the distance,
And the good that I can do.

GEORGE LINNAEUS BANKS

And now abideth . . . hope.

1 Corinthians 13:13

23
Abiding Hope

Underscore that word "abideth." It is a sturdy word. It is regretful that the word hope has become weakened in our language. For many, hope has come to mean mere wishful thinking. "I hope it won't rain tomorrow," we say. But *hope* is a strong soldier that marches side by side with the great words *faith and love.* Saint Paul bids us to "Put on the whole armour of God." He assures us that clothed with God's armor we can successfully contend against "the rulers of the darkness of this world," that we can face up to evil and keep standing. He lists the various parts of God's armor and he refers to the "helmet of salvation" (Ephesians 6:11–17). In another place the apostle tells us that the helmet is "the hope of salvation" (1 Thessalonians 5:8). Hope is strong enough to be included as part of God's armor.

No matter what happens, the Christian believes there is always a future. Hope causes us to realize there is always something ahead. Hope will have nothing to do with that defeatist nonsense—that there will always be wars, that man will always be selfish and sinful, that hunger and poverty can never be overcome. Hope is so sturdy, so real, and so aggressive that no matter what enemy it faces it does not back down—it "abideth."

Saint Paul tested hope in the burning fires of experience. He faced enough to shake the confidence of anybody, yet he found that in spite of every persecution, sickness, disappointment, and seeming defeat, hope still met the test. Nothing could destroy hope. "And now abideth . . . hope," he declared.

About sixteen centuries after Paul lived, a boy was born in Britain. Early in life he was stricken by a disease that grotesquely crippled him for life. Despite his suffering and handicaps, Alexander Pope came to be regarded by his generation as the greatest of English poets. This man who knew lifelong suffering wrote:

> Hope springs eternal in the human breast.

PART III

LOVE

24

It's Love or Nothing

The Bible, like a great mountain range, has certain high peaks. One of those peaks is 1 Corinthians 13. Just the reading of those words is an uplifting, cleansing experience. Countless poets have worked a lifetime to learn the art of putting words together to produce the harmony which Saint Paul has achieved in this masterpiece of his, but almost none have accomplished it.

When one's nerves are on edge, or one's spirit is depressed, the reading of this delightful poetry in prose makes one feel that life is worth the living, that there is good to be found.

More than the beauty of expression, however, the greatest of all Christian preachers is concerned about what he is saying. The content is more important than the beauty of the verse. He is speaking to people who are sick—people who are not living—people who can properly say, "I am nothing."

Nothing—what a startling word to apply to a person! *Nothing*—it means not anything, not at all—the opposite of something—of no account—of no value. *Nothing* even means nonexistent.

Who is a *nothing* person? ". . . and have not love, I am nothing."

"Though I speak with the tongues of men. . . ." As a student I studied English, Latin, Greek, and French. Suppose to those four had been added Russian, Chinese, German, Spanish, Italian, and the more than a thousand other languages and dialects of mankind. Suppose I had learned to speak every language perfectly. Then suppose further that I had communication with life beyond this world and could converse with the inhabitants of eternity. With that accomplishment I would say, "I am something."

"And though I have the gift of prophecy. . . ." Suppose God gave to me complete knowledge of all future events. Through the centuries, theologians have argued as to whether or not even God has this power. About the only agreed conclusion reached is that God knows all knowable things, but there is no final agreement as to what is knowable. If I had this awesome knowledge of the future, I would know more than any person who ever lived. I would say, "I am something."

"Understand all mysteries. . . ." In the city where I presently live is one of the world's finest hospitals for the treatment of cancer. I visit patients there frequently. Many have been cured. Many others have died. In spite of the vast research by thousands and thousands of highly trained specialists, much about cancer still remains a mystery. Suppose I knew all the answers, not only about cancer, but about every other mystery of man? I would know more than all the scientists have been able to learn. I could save the world all the money it will take to land a space ship on Mars and the countless other planets because I would know all that they would find. If I understood all mysteries, then I would say, "I am something."

"And all knowledge. . . ." As I write these words, I see on a shelf in my study an encyclopedia in many large volumes. I refer to these volumes from time to time, but I know I will never read every word in the entire set. Even if I did read every word, I would not retain in my mind all the knowledge in those books. Suppose I knew everything in every encyclopedia. Suppose all the knowledge contained in the world were stored up in my mind. I would say, "I am something."

"And though I have all faith, so that I could remove mountains. . . ." Perhaps Saint Paul is referring to Jesus' words, "If ye have faith as a grain of mustard seed, ye shall say unto this mountain, Remove hence to yonder place; and it shall remove: and nothing shall be impossible unto you" (Matthew 17:20). Here Jesus is saying that faith eliminates impossibilities. In this connection I think of Jesus' words, ". . . The things which are impossible with men are possible with God" (Luke 18:27). Suppose I did have the faith Jesus is talking about. I would then have the power of God. Truly, I could then say, "I am something."

Tongues, prophecy, mysteries, knowledge, and faith—as much as all this represents, I could have it all and still be nothing.

"And though I bestow all my goods to feed the poor. . . ." One is reminded of the young man who asked Jesus what he might do to gain eternal life. The reply was that he should keep the commandments. He wanted to know which commandments. So Jesus named some of them. "Thou shalt do no murder, Thou shalt not commit adultery, Thou shalt not steal, Thou shalt not bear false witness, Honor thy father and thy mother: and, Thou shalt love thy neighbor as thyself" (Matthew 19:18, 19).

Just the reading of that list makes me hang my head in shame. I stop right now to kneel with a prayer of repentance on my lips. Consider just the one in that list about false witness. We remember how Ananias and his wife, Sapphira, were struck dead for lying. Suppose everybody in the world today who ever told an untruth fell down and died. There would not be an Adam and Eve left to eat an apple.

This young man who was talking with Jesus said, "All these things I have kept from my youth up: what lack I yet?" Jesus knew that he had not kept all these commandments, but He did not correct him. The young man was obviously sincere in wanting the good life, and mercifully the Lord let the past be. So Jesus said to him, ". . . go and sell that thou hast, and give to the poor." The young man just could not bring himself to do it. So the end of the story is, ". . . he went away sorrowful" (vs. 21, 22).

We appreciate our possessions, and to give up everything we have is something most men just could not do.

"And though I give my body to be burned. . . ." In this connection, I think of certain saints across the centuries who have died at the stake. It takes courage and dedication beyond the capacity of ordinary men to be tied to a stake and allow the fire to be lighted to consume them. It would be a horrible way to die, but we have the record of many who have said, "Light the fire—I will die for my faith."

However, I think that Saint Paul had something else in mind. Burning as a means of putting one to death was probably not practiced in the first century. Crucifixion or stoning was the prevalent means. This was a day when slavery was commonly practiced. Just as ranchers brand cattle today, human beings were branded as slaves in that day. The hot iron was applied to their flesh, and those men wore that stigma the balance of their lives. "Though I give my body to become a branded slave. . . ." This is sacrifice in its most complete form. Yet—even such a sacrifice is profitless without love. "It profits me nothing."

Today we do not have "branded slaves," but we do brand ourselves as slaves. "I work hard at my job to support my family." "I keep the house, cook, scrub the floors, care for the children." "I have been singing in the choir, or teaching that class, or visiting prospective members every week." We can talk about how we have worked for others and for the Lord. ". . . without love, it profits me nothing."

If love is absent, all these other things are nothing. Without love, "I am nothing."

WHAT IS LOVE?

Actually Saint Paul does not define love. I doubt if anybody can. Someone once asked me to define the word *honey*. I studied about it and finally came up with this definition: "Honey is a sweet, syrupy substance manufactured by bees." I realize that is a very inadequate definition. I know I cannot really tell someone what honey is. I can give one some honey and that one can taste it.

Love defies definition, but it can be expressed. Saint Paul names the various expressions of love.

PATIENCE

"Love suffereth long"—is patient—endures long—is never tired of waiting. Love waits without murmuring. Love never gives up.

Once I was visiting a dear saint in the church, a fine woman who had lived more than eighty years. Few people came to see her. Her beloved husband had gone to the Father's House some years before. She was very lonely. Her arthritis was so bad that the movement of almost any part of her body was pain. Living for her had now become suffering. As we talked, she said to me, "Why do you suppose God is keeping me here?" I did not know what to answer, so we sat silently together for some moments. Then she began telling me about her son who was living a life far different from her teachings and from God. She thought out loud some of the wrong in her boy. Then she looked at me and said, "God is keeping me here to pray for my boy." Love is never tired of waiting.

Another story comes to mind. Somewhere I read of a son who again and again got into trouble. His father would bail him out until finally he had spent his life's savings. A neighbor said to the father, "If that were my boy, I would forget him." The father replied, "If he were your boy, I would forget him, too, but he is my boy."

Love learns to wait. The Psalmist said, "Yea, though I walk through the valley. . . ." Along the pathway of every life are some valleys. Disappointment, sorrow, illness, loss—these are some of the valleys. There are many more. Love underscores the word *through.* It knows the valley is not the end.

We recall how Jesus was being taken by those soldiers that night in Gethsemane. Simon Peter attacked with his sword, but Jesus told him to put the sword away. The Lord told how He could pray and the Father would give Him twelve legions of angels (Matthew 26:51–53). He could have fought force with force. Instead of force, he chose the slow method of love. He took the way of the cross—love suffereth long.

"For God so loved the world, that he gave his only begotten Son . . ." (John 3:16). This is the method He is always using. During World War II, many were heard to ask, "Why doesn't God kill Hitler?" But God was patient. As we see wrongs in our world, we wonder why God does not act, but love is patient. He never allows little men to make His decisions.

We become bothered by the faults in other people. Some in our own families may be very difficult to live with. We think of fellow workers, certain neighbors, different people in our city. When love is in our hearts, we are patient with those who make life hard for us.

Two short illustrations come to mind which show the advantage of patience. John Wesley's father once asked his wife, "How could you have the patience to tell that blockhead the same thing twenty times over?" "Why," she replied, "if I had told him but nineteen times, I should have lost all my labour."

When Da Vinci was painting his *Last Supper,* he was chided for standing hours before the canvas without making a stroke. He explained: "When I pause the longest, I make the most telling strokes with my brush."

Patience pays.

KINDNESS

". . . and is kind." Phillips' translation puts it: ". . . it looks for a way of being constructive." New World Translation says, ". . . and obliging." I like the word Wycliff uses—*benyngne* (benign).

I think one of the kindest acts in the story of Jesus happened at Jacob's well. Notice these words: ". . . Jesus therefore, being wearied with his journey, sat thus on the well: and it was about the sixth hour" (John 4:6).

The next verse begins: "There cometh a woman of Samaria to draw water: Jesus saith unto her. . . ."

For a Jewish man to speak to a Samaritan woman was beyond the bounds of decency. Worse, here was a woman whose reputation was quite tarnished. We can be sure she had been called many vile names. She had been snubbed again and again. She knew the meaning of hurt. But Jesus spoke to her. We read that His disciples ". . . marveled that he had talked with the woman" (v. 27). We may be sure they had plenty to say about it behind Jesus' back!

Not only that He spoke is important—also what He said. He did not condemn her for her actions. He did not berate her for her religious failures. He said, "Give me to drink" (v. 7). He allowed her to feel a sense of worth, to maintain some sense of dignity. This is an example of kindness.

Kindness is described as being love in action. It is those things we do. In this connection, we like to think of the well-known words of William Penn. He said, "I expect to pass through life but once. If therefore, there be any kindness I can show, or any good thing I can do to any fellow-being, let me do it now, and not defer or neglect it, as I shall not pass this way again."

Or, as Wordsworth, in "Tintern Abbey," put it:

> That best portion of a good man's life,
> His little, nameless, unremembered acts
> Of kindness and of love.

Few men in American industry have ever been paid a salary of as much as a million dollars a year. One of those men was Charles M. Schwab. It has been said that Andrew Carnegie did not pay Schwab a million dollars a year because he knew more about steel than anyone else knew. In fact, he had a hundred men under him who knew more about steel than he knew. Carnegie paid him a million dollars a year because he knew how to get along with other people. That ability, however, brought Schwab more than just financial gain. It brought him his deepest satisfactions in life.

When Mr. Schwab was past seventy years old, someone brought a nuisance suit against him. He easily won the suit in court, but before leaving the stand, he asked the judge's permission to say a few words. His comment that day is one of the most remarkable statements on kindness that we have recorded anywhere:

"I'd like to say, here, in a court of law, and speaking as an old man, that nine-tenths of my troubles are traceable to my being kind to others. Look, you young people, if you want to steer away from trouble, be hard-boiled. Be quick with a good loud no to anyone and everyone. If you follow this rule, you'll be seldom molested as you tread life's pathway. Except," and the great man paused, a grand smile lighting his kindly features, "except—you'll have no friends, you'll be lonely—and you won't have any fun!"

"What is real Good?"
I asked in musing mood.

Order, said the law court;
Knowledge, said the school;
Truth, said the wise man;
Pleasure, said the fool;
Love, said a maiden;
Beauty, said the page;
Freedom, said the dreamer;
Home, said the sage;
Fame, said the soldier;
Equity, the seer,

Spake my heart full sadly,
"The answer is not here."
Then within my bosom
Softly this I heard:
"Each heart holds the secret;
Kindness is the word."

JOHN BOYLE O'REILLY

ENVIETH NOT

"Love envieth not." Is not jealous. Is not possessive.

Here is one sin from which every one of us needs to be saved. There is something of the Prodigal Son's elder brother in all of us. He could love his brother as long as he was in the far country, as long as he was disgraced. But when he saw his father's arms about that boy, he was jealous. He would rather stay out in the darkness, then sit inside at the banquet table with his brother who had the good fortune of being restored.

Envy and jealousy can slip up on the best of people. In his book, *The Greatest of These,* Dr. Granville T. Walker recalls Oscar Wilde's story of how the devil was crossing the Libyan Desert when he met a number of his people tormenting a holy hermit. They tried to involve the hermit in sins of the flesh, tempting him in every way they knew to do, but to no avail. Steadfastly the sainted man shook off all their suggestions. Finally, after watching their failure in disgust, the devil whispered to the tempters, "What you do is too crude. Permit me one moment." Then the devil whispered to the holy man, "Your brother has just been made Bishop of Alexandria," and a scowl of malignant jealousy at once crowded the serene face of the hermit. "That," said the devil to his imps, "is the sort of thing which I recommend."

A fisherman friend told me that one never needs a top for his crab basket. If one of the crabs starts to climb up the side of the basket, the other crabs will reach up and pull it back down. Some people are a lot like crabs.

The reason love does not envy is because love is a spiritual quality. Envy is based on materialism. It might be possible to be envious of some spiritual gift in another person, but it is highly unlikely. I have never heard of a person who was envious of another person's goodness; rather would one be envious of another's position or wealth or talents.

In *The Deadly Game* by Will Manson there is a very revealing conversation:

> TRAPP I've been around, all right. But as far as I can see, people are about the same wherever you go.
>
> GUSTAVE You feel that we all have a certain common humanity which is more important than individual differences?
>
> TRAPP Well, actually I was thinking in terms of sales technique. When you're trying to sell a piece of merchandise, it doesn't matter if the customer is rich or poor, young or old, male or female—there are three things you always have to make him believe. One: that he is getting the product for a lot less than it's worth. Two: that all the people he looks up to in the world have got one. And three: that his best friends are going to burn with jealousy because he has one.
>
> GUSTAVE In short, greed, envy, and condescension—these, in your opinion, are the mainsprings of human conduct?

The tragedy is that the road of envy and jealousy fails so completely to satisfy. Arthur Miller wrote a play entitled *Death of a Salesman.* Two friends are talking:

> BIFF Are you content, Hap? You're a success, aren't you. Are you content?
>
> HAPPY No!
>
> BIFF Why? You're making money, aren't you?
>
> HAPPY All I can do now is wait for the merchandise manager to die. And suppose I get to be merchandising manager? He's a good friend of mine, and he just built a terrific estate on Long Island. And he lived there two months and sold it, and now he's building another one. He can't enjoy it once it's finished. And I know that's just what I would do. I

don't know what . . . I'm working for. Sometimes I sit in my apartment—all alone. And I think of the rent I'm paying. And it's crazy. But then, it's what I always wanted. My own apartment, a car . . . And still . . . I'm lonely.

Envy and jealousy can never possibly be satisfied. There was a farmer who was miserable because he could not buy the land adjoining his, but he would have to have all the land in all the world to really accomplish that. But love does satisfy because it is not thinking of itself. A person can love who owns nothing and yet feel happy and have a sense of well-being.

Rudyard Kipling, the brilliant English poet, was speaking to a graduating class at McGill University. He advised the graduates not to care too much for money or power or fame; for, he said, "Someday you will meet a man who cares for none of these things . . . and then you will know how poor you are."

HUMILITY

". . . vaunteth not itself, is not puffed up." ". . . Not forward and self-assertive, nor boastful and conceited." ". . . Does not make a vain display of itself, and does not boast." "Love is not proud." "It does not brag." "Love is not out for display." "Love makes no parade." "It is neither anxious to impress nor does it cherish inflated ideas of its own importance." "It does not put on airs." "Love has no high opinion of itself, love has no pride."

Envy and jealousy is one side of the coin. Boasting and conceit is the other side of the same coin. Both desire to be above one's fellowmen—one by pulling the other fellow down, the other by pushing oneself above.

Love learns to be humble, and humility is learned in different ways. One of life's pathways to humility is through being hurt. In the second act of Dore Schary's *Sunrise at Campobello,* Franklin D. Roosevelt is saying:

> Eleanor, I must say this—once to someone. Those first days at Campobello when I started, I had despair—deep, sick despair. It wasn't the pain—there was much more of that later on when they straightened the tendons in my legs. No, not the pain—it was the sense that perhaps I'd never get up again. Like a crab lying on its back. I'd look down at my fingers and exert every thought to get them to move. I'd send down orders to my legs and toes—they didn't obey . . . I turned to my faith, Babs—for strength to endure. I feel I have to go through this fire for some reason. Eleanor, it's a hard way to learn humility—but I've been learning by crawling. I know what it meant—you must learn to crawl before you can walk.

Sometimes life has a way of putting us on our backs in order to force us to look up. It is in looking up that we achieve this virtue of love—humility.

An amateur artist may paint a picture which he thinks is so good that, as he looks over his creation, he can easily become "puffed up." But let that same artist stand for an hour before one of the masterpieces of Hoffman or Rosetti or Muller or Hunt or Da Vinci or Rubens, and then his self-satisfactions melt away, and instead of being boastful and conceited, he finds new inspiration to greater effort.

A budding poet may be very proud of himself because of some verses he has written. He may become very anxious to impress others with his own genius and think of himself as having every right to put on airs. But let that budding poet refer again to Homer or Milton or Dante or Shakespeare or Chaucer or Byron or Scott or Burns or Gray. Then the temptation to vaunt himself easily is overcome.

The musician might feel inclined toward vain display until he hears again the music of Beethoven or Bach or Schubert or Handel.

Similarly, we Christians have a tendency toward thinking of ourselves more highly than we ought to think. Goodness is one of the graces we quickly and easily appropriate unto ourselves. Self-righteousness likes to parade itself. But when we stand before Martin Luther or Saint Francis or Augustine or Loyola or John Wesley or David Livingstone or William Booth or Booker T. Washington—or more especially, when we stand before Him of whom men could say, "Thou art the Christ, the Son of the living God"—then we make no vain display of ourselves.

Thinking along this line, it is easy to see what Phillips Brooks meant when he said, "The true way to be humble . . . is to stand at your real height against some high nature. . . ."

Instead of belittling one, true humility lifts and enlarges one. In a church at Copenhagen there is the famous statue by Thorwaldsen, depicting Christ extending the invitation, "Come unto me." Someone was standing before that statue and was obviously disappointed. Sensing that disappointment, one who was familiar with the statue said to the visitor, "You must go close to it, sir. You must kneel down and look up, if you wish to see Christ's face."

It is impossible to see Christ in any other way. There is a very good reason why we kneel to pray. The very act of kneeling is important.

When love possesses a person, that person has a sense of being one member of the family of God and thinks of all men as precious.

One day, when Toscanini was conducting a rehearsal at the Metropolitan Opera House, a soprano soloist, who was famous and temperamental, objected to the maestro's suggestions. "I am the star of this performance," she exclaimed. "Madame," Toscanini replied quietly, "in this performance there are no stars." In the performance of love, there are no stars.

No one has said it better than the shepherd's boys in Bunyan's *Pilgrim's Progress:*

> He that is down need fear no fall.
> He that is low, no pride:
> He that is humble, ever shall
> Have God to be his guide.

GOOD MANNERS

". . . doth not behave itself unseemly." ". . . does not behave unbecomingly." ". . . is never rude." ". . . doth not behave indecently." "Love is not ill-mannered." "Love has good manners." "Love's ways are always fair." ". . . never haughty."—Reading the various versions of this love chapter, we are thankful for the various meanings which are revealed to us.

This is considered one of the minor attributes of love. The more we think about it, however, the larger it grows in importance. John Galsworthy put this expression of love in its proper place of importance when he wrote in *Maid in Waiting,* "All our institutions, religion, marriage, treaties, the law, and the rest, are simply forms of consideration for others necessary to secure consideration for self."

Indeed, the success of people living together, in what we call society, is based in no small measure on such simple things as politeness, tact, and good manners. The words *gentleman* and *lady* denote qualities both of actions and of character which are extremely desirable—yea, even essential for people in association with each other.

Such acts as holding a chair or opening a car door for a lady, saying, *please,* or *thank you,* writing a note of appreciation, observing good table manners, allowing someone to enter a door ahead of you, saying something nice about a person when you introduce him or her, not contradicting someone telling a story, holding a lady's coat, saying how much you enjoyed being with someone, cleanliness of body and of speech—and the list could go on and on—these so-called little things do make a difference in people's lives. Someone has well said:

> Politeness is to do and say,
> The kindest thing in the kindest way.

One of the best stories I have heard along this line came from Rolland W. Schloerb. A man was once impressed by the courtesy of the conductor toward the passengers on a streetcar. After the crowd had thinned out, he spoke to the conductor about it. "Well," the conductor explained, "about five years ago I read in the paper about a man who was included in a will just because he was polite. 'What in the world?' I thought. 'It might happen to me.' So I started treating passengers like people. And it makes me feel so good that now I don't care if I never get a million dollars."

This illustrates one of the main advantages of all the attributes of love—not only does it make for happiness in others, it comes back to bless our own lives.

We have heard the phrase "mind your manners" since we were children. In most instances, people who are reading these words do that, especially when we are in public. Sometimes we forget it, however, when we are in private. It is sad but true that often we are the rudest to the ones we love the most. We all know that we should be at our best in the circle of those whose love means the most to us.

My good friend, Dr. Robert H. Schuller says it well:

> Of first importance—find out the sensitive area in your mate's life. There is something that will offend him that you would never suspect would be offensive. Everybody has his pet peeves. For myself, it was when my wife neglected to put the cap on the toothpaste tube the first couple of weeks after we were married.
>
> Husbands, find out what about your life bothers your wife most. Wives, find out what about your life bothers your husband most.
>
> Chances are you do not realize what about you is most offensive to your mate. I recently played the marriage game with my wife. I asked her what habit or behavior pattern about my life was most disagreeable to her. I was positive that I knew what her answer would be. I had about three negative factors in my life that I expected her to mention. Instead she named something that I never thought bothered her at all! We turned the game around and played it the other way. And she never guessed what qualities in her life I found most potentially disagreeable.
>
> This is probably due to the fact that we just really never know ourselves as others know us. Play the game. Find out what in your life is most disagreeable to your mate.
>
> Then by all means use your head and know that common decency and good manners would dictate that you correct or neutralize that negative quality promptly and permanently.
>
> It may be some simple little habit. But remember that—

It's the little things we do
And the minor words we say
That make or break the beauty
Of the average passing day.

UNSELFISH

". . . seeketh not her own." ". . . does not insist on its own way." ". . . does not pursue selfish advantage."

Now we arrive at the very highest expression of love. Our Lord best expressed it when He declared His purpose in life was "not to be ministered unto, but to minister . . ." (Matthew 20:28).

Psychologists speak of the "narcissus complex," which means an extreme self-love. This comes out of a story in Greek mythology. Narcissus, a very handsome young man, one day looked into the quiet waters of a pool and saw the reflection of himself. He completely fell in love with that self-reflection. To some extent, this happens to all of us and, as Oscar Wilde said in *An Ideal Husband,* "To love one's self is the beginning of a lifelong romance."

Love is so strong it can overcome even the instinct of self. There come to all our minds numerous stories of how people have sacrificed in so many ways, even their own lives, because they loved someone more than themselves. One of the best of such stories is recorded by Victor Hugo in *Ninety-Three.*

> After the revolution, a French mother was driven from her home with her three children including an infant. She had wandered through the woods and fields for several days. She and her three children had lived on roots and leaves. On the third morning, they had hidden in some bushes on the approach of some soldiers and a sergeant.

The sergeant ordered a soldier to find out what was stirring in the bushes; he prodded the mother and her three children out. They were brought to the sergeant's side, and he saw in an instant that they were starving; he gave them a long loaf of brown French bread. The mother took it eagerly, like a famished animal, broke it into two pieces, giving one piece to one child and the other to the second child.

"She has kept none for herself," grumbled the sergeant.

"Because she is not hungry," said a soldier.

"Because she is a mother," said the sergeant.

This is what Saint Paul meant when he said, ". . . love does not seek its own."

Love always gives, and (let it be emphasized) love always has something to give. A classic example is the story of Peter and John on their way to church. A crippled beggar was sitting at the temple gate asking for alms. This man had been crippled since birth and had become a professional beggar. One thing he had learned was that church people were the best people from whom to beg. People who worship God are people who give.

As Peter and John approached, the beggar asked them for alms. Peter said, "Silver and gold have I none." He might have prolonged the list of things he did not have. Neither did he have a formal education, nor much social standing in the community. He was a busy man and lacked much time to spare. He could easily have passed the beggar by. But Peter had a loving concern in his heart, so he added, "But such as I have give I thee!" (Acts 3:6). His was the positive mood. There is no power in what one does not have, or cannot do, or does not believe.

Once after Dwight L. Moody had finished a sermon, a man said to him, "Mr. Moody, in your sermon I noted that you made eleven mistakes in grammar." Mr. Moody replied,

"Very likely I did. My early education was faulty. I often wish I had received more schooling. But I am using all the grammar I know in the service of Christ."

We all have limitations and we can use our limitations as an excuse not to give. Peter, however, wanted to give and was not looking for an excuse not to. That is the difference love makes. Peter was willing to give what he could in the way he could. Not having money, he thought about his faith and he gave that. He said,"In the name of Jesus Christ of Nazareth rise up and walk" (v. 6).

Then he gave something else: "And he took him by the right hand . . ." (v. 7). He gave him loving fellowship.

There is a story that Ivan S. Turgenev, the Russian writer, met a beggar who asked him for money. "I felt in my pockets," he said, "but there was nothing there. The beggar waited, and his outstretched hand twitched and trembled slightly. Embarrassed and confused, I seized his dirty hand and pressed it. 'Do not be angry with me, brother,' I said, 'I have nothing with me.' The beggar raised his bloodshot eyes and smiled. 'You called me brother,' he said, 'that was indeed a gift.' "

As a result of Peter's giving, the story ends with the beggar going with them into the temple, ". . . walking, and leaping, and praising God" (v. 8). When love gives it always blesses.

We think of Sister Kenny, who was a nurse in the bush country of Australia many years ago. One day she wired the chief surgeon of a hospital about a strange disease which had struck four children. He wired back, INFANTILE PARALYSIS, NO KNOWN CURE, DO BEST YOU CAN. A year later she told this physician, "There were two more cases even worse than the first four, but all six are well now."

"Splendid," said the doctor, "how badly are they crippled?"

"Why, they are not crippled," she replied, "they are entirely normal."

He was delighted, but very much surprised. He asked, "What did you do?"

Her answer was, "I used what I had—water, heat, blankets, and my own hands."

She found the way by giving what she had. "Such as I have I give" is the autobiography of love.

SELF-CONTROL

". . . is not easily provoked." ". . . nor blaze out in passionate anger." "Love . . . is not irritable." "It is not touchy or fretful." ". . . not quick to take offence." "It is not exasperated." The word in the King James Version is *provoked,* but as we read other versions, we have that word enlarged on and made clearer.

It is so easy to think of anger as one of the minor sins. Indeed, it is easy to even think of anger as a virtue. We have heard someone say, "I have a temper," as if that is something to be proud of. Every person has a temper, but not every person has learned the art of self-control. What Saint Paul is talking about is the fact that love has the power to so master one's emotions that it is always in control.

Jesus told a story about a man who had two sons. One of those sons became a prodigal who ". . . wasted his substance with riotous living" (Luke 15:13). He committed various sins of the flesh, which we have heard condemned again and again. But that boy eventually ended up at his father's table.

It was the other son who was left out in the darkness at the end of the story. He was the one who was lost. Why? This elder brother had many qualities which we admire. He never did many of the bad things his brother did. He was a faithful worker in his father's fields—yet Jesus did not have one kind word for him.

When his prodigal brother returned home, the story says, "... he was angry and would not go in ..." (v. 28). Why was he angry? Simply because he lacked love in his heart. Notice the pronouns in this sentence: "... thou never gavest me a kid, that I might make merry with my friends" (v. 29)—*me—I—my.* In complaining to his father he said, "... This thy son ..." (v. 30). Gently the father tries to correct him with the phrase, "... This thy brother ..." (v. 32), but he would not accept that relationship of love. The alternative was jealous anger. This was the boy who was lost.

Go over the roll of any church and you find names of people who have quit. Some quit out of indifference, but so often you come to names of people who have quit because something upset them. I heard a man explaining why he could not agree with certain positions his pastor took. Some of the things his pastor said in his sermons were quite offensive to this man. But then he added, "I am not going to let any preacher run me out of my church." There is a man whose love for God and his church transcended any irritations or provocations he might have had.

For one who would learn the fine art of self-control, I have four suggestions:

(1) *Determine your most vulnerable point.* I have known people who could endure prolonged pain, yet would go to pieces under a criticism. Impatience is the problem of many. Some cannot stand it, if everything doesn't go his or her way. At this point, we need to consider our prejudices. The list could be extended as to why people get upset, but the important thing is for each of us to determine our own Achilles heel.

(2) *Try to understand other people.* For example, suppose some person is rude to you. It may be a clerk in a store, or someone you work with, or an inconsiderate automobile driver, or one of your neighbors, or one of your children, or your wife or your husband. Instead of becoming irritated or angry, ask the question: "I wonder why that person acts that way?" That question could have various answers. Maybe that person is sick, or has experienced a deep sorrow, or has been mistreated by someone else, or any number of reasons. If we know a person, it is much easier to take a loving attitude.

(3) *Try to understand your own emotions.* When you feel yourself getting upset, try to understand why. This can lead to most helpful self-examinations. Epictetus said, "Reckon the days in which you have not been angry. I used to be angry every day; now every other day; then every third and fourth day; and if you miss it so long as thirty days, offer a sacrifice of thanksgiving to God."

Dr. J. Wallace Hamilton, one of the most gifted and beloved ministers America has known, tells a wonderful story in his book, *Ride the Wild Horses.*

As a boy, the gifted Negro tenor, Roland Hayes, heard an old Negro minister preach a sermon on Christ before Pilate. The preacher contrasted two kinds of power confronting each other. Pilate, irked by the silence of Jesus, cried, "Why don't you answer me? Don't you know I have power?" The illiterate old preacher went on to say, "No matter how angry the crowd got, He never said a mumberlin' word, not a word." Years later, at the peak of fame with his golden voice, Roland Hayes stood before a Nazi audience in Berlin's Beethoven Hall. The audience was hostile, ugly, scornful of a Negro daring to sing at the center of Aryan culture. He was greeted with a chorus of Nazi hisses, growing louder and more ominous; for ten minutes Hayes stood there in silence at the piano, resentment swelling up in him like an irresistible tide. And then he remembered the sermon of long ago: "He never said a mumberlin' word, not a word." He shouted back no words born in anger; he kept his head, for he knew that the ultimate power was on his side, not theirs. He stood there and prayed, silently, and the quiet dignity of his courage conquered the savage spirits in his audience, and in hushed pianissimo he began to sing a song of Schubert's. He won, without so much as "a mumberlin' word."

(4) *Develop companionship with God.* I have played golf with a certain friend many times. I have been told that on the golf course he easily becomes frustrated and, after a bad shot, will use loud profanity. In fact, he is noted for this behavior. Yet, in all the times we have played together, I have never seen him lose his temper or express a word of profanity. I asked him about this one day and he replied, "When I am with my preacher I control myself."

Suppose one realized that he or she is in God's presence at all times. What a marvelous difference that would make! Mrs. Fulton Oursler said that when she felt herself getting provoked, she would count up to ten. Then one day she thought of the first ten words of the Lord's Prayer. Now instead of counting up to ten, she slowly says, "Our Father which art in heaven, Hallowed be thy name."

"He that is slow to anger is better than the mighty; and he that ruleth his spirit than he that taketh a city" (Proverbs 16:32).

I do not ask for any crown
But that which all may win;
Nor try to conquer any world
Except the one within.
Be Thou my guide until I find
Led by a tender hand,
The happy kingdom in myself
And dare to take command.

LOUISA MAY ALCOTT

FORGIVES AND FORGETS

"... thinketh no evil." "... never resentful." "... nor does she reckon up her wrongs." "It never harbors evil thoughts." "It is not touchy." "... will hardly even notice when others do us wrong." "... does not imagine evil." "... does not brood over an injury." Again—it is wonderful how the various translators illuminate the meaning of God's words.

One of life's temptations is to wear our feelings "on our sleeve." In some strange way, getting our feelings hurt ministers to our ego. To forgive or forget a wrong toward us is in a sense to surrender. It is our natural inclination to fight back.

Let me recount here a personal experience which has been real good for me. When I was in the fourth grade in school, the superintendent of that school did me a wrong. I knew it then and I know it now. He fell out with my father about something and he took it out on me. We moved away from that town, and for years I did not see him again.

Then, during my first pastorate out of the seminary, we crossed paths again. This was during a period of depression, when jobs were hard to get. If a school board had a vacancy, they received a stack of applications. This man had lost his job the year before and had been trying all the summer to find another place, but without success. Just a few days before school was to begin, the superintendent in the town where I was living resigned. This man applied for that place. I heard about it and I said to myself, "It has been a long time."

I knew that as soon as I told my friends on the school board what I knew about that man—and some other things I thought up about him—they would not hire him. I went out to get in my car to go see some of the board members, and suddenly it came over me what I had done. Here I was, out trying to represent Him who was nailed to the Cross, and I was carrying a grudge. That realization was a humiliating experience. I went back into my house, knelt by my bedside and said, "Lord, if you will forgive me of this, I will never be guilty any more." That experience and that promise are among the best things that ever happened in my life.

Love just cannot be sensitive, touchy, unforgiving. A minister tells of a lady in his church who was on a committee. It was announced that a meeting of the committee was to be held in another woman's home who was also on the committee. The lady said to the minister, "After what she did, I will not set foot in her house."

The minister asked when she joined that church. She told him twenty-seven years ago. Then he began to name each one of the ministers who had been at that church during those years. He pointed out that each one was a capable and faithful preacher of the gospel. Then he said, "You mean to say that for twenty-seven years in this church, you have sat here as the love of Christ was preached and now you say you will not 'set foot in her house'?" Then sadly he added, "Lady, what have you heard in church?"

It is so easy to keep account of wrongs against us, to be too sensitive, to look for evil when none was intended. But love almost refuses to be insulted or to be hurt. There is a toughness and a strength about love that protects one's heart and feelings, like a suit of armor protects the body.

IS NOT GLAD BECAUSE OF WRONG

". . . rejoiceth not in iniquity, but rejoiceth in the truth." ". . . never glad when others go wrong." ". . . Takes no pleasure in other people's sins."

Over and over we have heard the saying, "Love is blind." That is not true. Love has eyes that can see, and love is aware. But let it be emphasized that love also has eyelids, and sometimes love chooses to close its eyes and not see. Love looks for the good instead of the bad, and when someone does wrong, love is always genuinely regretful.

A friend of mine, who raises turkeys, told me that when a turkey is wounded and gets a spot of blood on its feathers, the other turkeys will peck at that spot until they literally peck the wounded turkey to death. Alas—people can be like that. Here is a place where we must be very careful. It is so easy to be glad when someone goes wrong. The reason is that it ministers to our own conceits. We have not done that particular wrong, and that makes us feel self-righteous.

Gossip is one sin for which restitution cannot be made most of the time. A woman confessed to Philip Neri that she had been spreading slanderous reports. He said, "Go into the market, buy a chicken, pluck out its feathers, and throw them away, and return to me." She obeyed. "Now go back and bring all the feathers you have scattered," said Neri.

"That is impossible," said the woman.

"Yes," said Neri, "your words of slander have been carried about in every direction, and you cannot recall them."

Four reasons come to mind as to why we are glad when others go wrong:

(1) Being conscious of our own sins, we take comfort in the fact that we are not the only ones who have done wrong.

(2) Because we are jealous. Sometimes we secretly in our hearts would like to commit the same sins we condemn, but we lack the nerve, or the opportunity, or our own consciences will not let us.

(3) We do not know all the facts about the other person. On the Cross, Jesus prayed, "Father forgive them . . ." Why did He pray that prayer? Because He knew the limitations of their own understanding: ". . . for they know not what they do" (Luke 23:34). If we really knew the other person, we would be much kinder.

(4) Because we lack love in our hearts. I like the story about the father who overheard one of his sons say, "If you do that, father won't love you." He said to his children, "I shall always love you. When you do what is right, I love you with a glad heart, and when you do what is wrong, I still love you, but with a heart full of sorrow."

James Whitcomb Riley said it beautifully in some verses entitled, "Let Something Good Be Said":

> When over the fair frame of friend or foe
>   The shadow of disgrace shall fall, instead
> Of words of blame, or proof of so and so,
>   Let something good be said.
>
> Forget not that no fellow-being yet
>   May fall so low but love may lift his head;
> Even the cheek of shame with tears is wet,
>   If something good be said.
>
> No generous heart may vainly turn aside
>   In ways of sympathy, no soul so dead
> But may awaken strong and glorified,
>   If something good be said.

And so I charge ye, by the thorny crown,
　　And by the cross on which the Saviour bled,
And by your own soul's hope of fair renown,
　　Let something good be said.

These words, "Rejoiceth not in iniquity, but rejoiceth in the truth," are well illustrated by the story of Xanthus ordering his servant, Aesop, to provide the best things in the market for his guests. Each course consisted of tongue with different sauces. When Xanthus complained, Aesop said, "Nothing is better than tongue. It is the bond of civil society, the organ of truth and reason, the instrument of our praise of God."

The next day Xanthus ordered the worst things in the market, and Aesop provided tongue. When reprimanded, Aesop said, "The tongue is the worst thing. It is lies, blasphemies, the source of division and war." The tongue can be the worst part of man; or it can be the best part.

This attribute of love is summed up in a story from the first book in the Bible. Let us read it together:

> And Noah began to be an husbandman, and he planted a vineyard: And he drank of the wine, and was drunken; and he was uncovered within his tent. And Ham, the father of Canaan, saw the nakedness of his father, and told his two brethren without. And Shem and Japheth took a garment, and laid it upon both their shoulders, and went backward, and covered the nakedness of their father; and their faces were backward, and they saw not their father's nakedness. And Noah awoke from his wine, and knew what his younger son had done unto him. And he said, Cursed be Canaan; a servant of servants shall he be unto his brethren. And he said, Blessed be the Lord God of Shem; and Canaan shall be his servant. God shall enlarge

Japheth, and he shall dwell in the tents of Shem; and Canaan shall be his servant.

Genesis 9:20–27

It has always been to the credit of Shem and Japheth that they refused to look upon their father's shame.

SUPPORTING STATEMENTS

In the foregoing phrases we have Saint Paul's analysis of love. Then comes a series of strong statements which support and strengthen his exalted view of love.

LOVE WILL ENDURE

"... Beareth all things, believeth all things, hopeth all things, endureth all things. Love never faileth; but whether there be prophecies, they shall fail; whether there be knowledge, it shall vanish away." —Love is the one thing that will last, no matter what happens and even when everything else is gone.

John Steinbeck said it well in *East of Eden:* "We have only one story. All novels, all poetry, are built on the never-ending contest in ourselves of good and evil. And it occurs to me that evil must constantly respawn, while good, while virtue, is immortal. Vice has always a new fresh young face, while virtue is venerable as nothing else in the world is."

LOVE WAITS FOR THE FULL ANSWER

"For we know in part, and we prophesy in part. But when that which is perfect is come, then that which is in part shall be done away ... For now we see through a glass, darkly: but then face to face: now I know in part; but then shall I know even as also I am known."

These words strike a responsive chord in every human heart. There are so many times when we wonder why certain things happened. Why sickness—handicaps—disappointment—wrecks—war—death, and all the others. Sooner or later each of us will ask, "Why?" and will realize we do ". . . see through a glass darkly." We just cannot find an answer.

One thing to be said is that life's possibilities come in pairs: goodness and evil, short and tall, strong and weak, hot and cold—and also pain and pleasure. The existence of one assures the possibility of the other. Every possible blessing is also a possible pain.

Take love out of the human heart and you will also be taking away most of our capacity to be hurt, but that is too high a price to pay. At times we must resign ourselves to our lack of understanding, but we find our strength in our faith that God knows and that God cares. The Psalmist put two wonderful statements together: "He healeth the broken in heart, and bindeth up their wounds. He telleth the number of stars; he calleth them all by their names" (Psalms 147:3, 4). That is, the God who watches over all the universe also cares for each of His children.

There are some things we will not understand but we have the blessed promise that someday it will all be cleared up for us: "Now I know in part, but then shall I know. . . ." I quote and I believe the words:

Not now but in the coming years,
It may be in a better land;
We'll learn the meaning of our tears,
And there, sometime, we'll understand.

MAXWELL N. CORNELIUS

I mention another thought at this point. The fact that "Now we see through a glass, darkly" can be very merciful. We would not want to see clearly the future, even if we could. We are satisfied to live each day as it comes.

LOVE GROWS UP

"When I was a child, I spake as a child, I understood as a child, I thought as a child: but when I became a man, I put away childish things."

Life brings no greater blessing than a child, but it is a heartbreaking tragedy for a child to never develop, physically or mentally. And some people never mature. Let us list several characteristics of little children:

(1) Children become very upset over any personal hurt. If pins prick the flesh, they will cry as if deadly wounded. They are not the most concerned about the suffering of others, they weep mostly for themselves.

(2) Children want to be the center of attention. They are jealous of all about them. They are willing to play, if they can choose the game. They demand applause and appreciation.

(3) Children have to be taught to be thankful. Gratitude for them does not come naturally. They take all the blessings of life as a matter of course.

(4) Children owe nobody anything. Their attitude is to get all they can but they have little obligation to any person. They rarely think of what they owe their parents or the society in which they live.

(5) Children are completely self-centered. They live in a world that revolves about themselves.

When one grows up (puts away childish things), it does not mean that tears never come to his eyes. It does mean that tears are reserved for causes that deserve them and never given to petty trifles. A mature person can and does weep over his own personal hurts, but more often the tears of love are for the hurts of others.

When one grows up, he still appreciates approval by others, but still goes on living and working and serving even when there is no recognition by others. Also, gratitude and appreciation of others is one of the flowers of mature love. Love is always glad to say, "Thank you." Also, love feels a deep sense of obligation to others. Saint Paul said, "I am debtor both to the Greeks, and to the Barbarians; both to the wise and the unwise" (Romans 1:14). He felt he owed something, not only to those who blessed him, but also to those in need. Love feels its obligation to serve.

Love puts away childish things—it grows up.

THE GRAND CLIMAX

Saint Paul closes this, the most complete statement on love in existence, with a grand climax in verse 13: "And now abideth faith, hope, love, these three: but the greatest of these is love."

Underscore that word *abideth.* Make a list of the things people are seeking today, and we see that so many of these are temporary—clothes that will be out of style next year, cars that will wear out, treasures that "moth and rust doth corrupt." So often we are disappointed in the things we possess because we realize they are for such a short duration. Every material possession will one day be lost; physical strength will one day become weakness; the years will steal away our beauty. The most brilliant career will come to an end. The most thunderous applause will die into silence. The satisfaction we have in our possessions today is no guarantee that we will be satisfied tomorrow.

How much better to possess some things that *abideth*—things that will endure no matter what happens. Saint Paul names three things that we can hold onto forever: faith, hope, and love.

FAITH

Without faith, life is a difficult journey. Without faith, we are never quite sure of ourselves. Without faith, it is difficult to make decisions. Without faith, we are afraid to dare, to dream, to adventure. Failing to possess faith, we look at our fellow man with suspicion and cynicism. We miss the comfort and stimulation of real friendships. We think the world is against us. We lose our enthusiasm for living.

Without faith, we lose our great ideals and purposes, and life takes on a lower tone. Without faith, we become possessed with a what's-the-use attitude.

There are many definitions of faith, but essentially it means two things: first, to continue to believe no matter what happens. One of the grandest statements Saint Paul made was this one: "I have kept the faith." Life dealt harshly with him, but through it all, he held fast to certain firm convictions. He was faithful to his highest principles, and in being faithful, he never lost his faith.

The other part of faith is that when we face up to life and know that we are unable to conquer life in our own strength, we can depend on a higher help. Faith means three things about God:

(1) God created this world. It also means that God controls this world. For a time it may seem that evil will triumph, but remember, "This is my Father's world."

(2) Faith means God cares. There come times when one

feels forgotten and deserted, left out and alone. I wrote a boy who was located thousands of miles away. He wrote back, "Your letter made me feel that I had not been forgotten." This assurance gives inspiration for living.

(3) Faith means God is working with us and not just watching us from afar. This does not mean that everything that happens is good, or according to His will. Sometimes God's will can be temporarily defeated. But God continues to work, and God will triumph.

In this connection, we recall a conversation from *The Big Fisherman* by Lloyd C. Douglas.

> "Don't forget," admonished Peter, "that we couldn't understand why he wanted to leave Canaan and come to Capernaum."
>
> "That was different," mumbled Thomas. "He felt that he was urgently needed there." "Maybe he feels that he is now needed elsewhere," observed Andrew, to which James added, "I don't believe he cares very much whether we understand him or not."
>
> "You are right, Jimmy," rumbled old Bartholomew. "He's teaching us to have faith in him."
>
> "But—can't a man have faith—and understanding, too?" argued Thomas.
>
> "No!" declared Bartholomew, bluntly. "That's what faith is for, my son! It's for when we can't understand!"
>
> "That's true!" approved Peter. "When a man understands, he doesn't need any faith."
>
> "I don't like to be kept in the dark," put in Philip.
>
> "If a man has enough faith," replied Peter, "he can find his way in the dark—with faith as his lamp."

Even in the midst of confusion, doubt, and failure of understanding, faith abideth.

HOPE

Hope is something else that will abide. Many people have so watered down hope that it represents little more than wishful thinking. But hope is something big and strong and sturdy. It is a firm expectation based on certain fundamental truths and actions. Hope is never a substitute for clear thinking and hard work. On the contrary, hope leads one to think and to work.

When one becomes discouraged, when life looks utterly dark, when all one's plans have failed, then there is a choice of one of three ways out.

(1) There is the way of the fool. The Bible tells us, "The fool hath said in his heart, there is no God . . ." (Psalms 14:1). This way looks at difficult situations and sees nothing but hopelessness. Seeing no hope, this person simply says, "I will quit . . . I don't like this job, I'll get another one . . . This thrill has let me down, I will seek another one . . . There are some problems in my marriage, I will break it up . . . I cannot face this situation, I will run away from it." Having no hope, a person can have nothing to hold onto.

(2) A second way to face the troubles of life is the cynic's way. It is a little better than the fool's way but not much better. The cynic believes everything turns out bad. "This is just my luck," he says. "There is no joy in life for me; I'll just bear it the best I can." The cynic never expects much, and thus he is never very disappointed. He is simply resigned to life.

(3) A third way to face life is the way of hope. Of course, there will be disappointments and setbacks, but hope sees the sunshine following the storm. God gave us ears to hear with because there is music to be heard. The Christian believes that. Also, he believes God gave us eyes because there is beauty to be seen. Also, he believes God gave us

the ability to hope because there is something finer and better ahead, and if we keep going, we shall find it.

Hope, like a gleaming taper's light,
Adorns and cheers our way:
And still, as darker grows the night,
Emits a brighter ray.

OLIVER GOLDSMITH
The Captivity

LOVE

Love is the third thing that *abideth.* But it is more than just the third thing: "The greatest of these is love." And, love is what this part of the book is all about.

25

Love Overcomes Destructive Emotions

"Perfect love casteth out fear," said Saint John in the long ago (1 John 4:18). And modern medicine and psychology have finally caught up with the Bible and confirmed that truth. John is talking about the two strongest emotions of the human system—love and fear—and he says love has the power to destroy fear.

Physicians today tell us that from 50 to 75 percent of all of our sickness is caused by our emotions. Emotion is simply the ability to feel. Keep telling yourself that you feel sick, and you will be sick. If you are sick, more than half of the time your sickness will be cured simply by convincing yourself that you feel well.

We have physical bodies and we also have feelings or emotions. Basically all of our emotions are good, but if any of them get out of control, then they are bad. Like fire. Fire is one of the greatest benefactors of man. But uncontrolled fire can burn up a man's house, and even the man himself.

There are four main groups of destructive emotions. Actually, even these emotions are good as long as we can control them, but when we let them get out of hand, they make us sick in many ways.

(1) There is the *fear* group, including anxiety, worry, and apprehension.

(2) *Anger* is the father of another group of destructive emotions. Some of the children of anger are hostility, resentment, envy, jealousy, and hatred. However, anger is closely related to fear because we do not feel hostile toward a person until we become afraid that person can hurt us in some way.

(3) A third group of destructive emotions is headed up by what we feel as a *sense of failure.* This leads to such things as discouragement, depressed moods, and various guilt feelings. Without this family of emotions, there would be no repentance, but they also lead to self-destruction.

(4) *Pride* is the captain of another army of sickening emotions, including prejudice, selfishness, self-consciousness, and conceit.

When Saint John says, "Perfect love casteth out fear," I think that by fear he has in mind *all* of the destructive emotions, because they are all a part of fear or stem from fear. And when he talks about love, he means all of the healing emotions, because love is the basis of them all.

There is faith, which makes us believe. And hope, which keeps us looking upward and forward. ". . . but the greatest of these is love," said Saint Paul (1 Corinthians 13:13). And God's Book tells us that if you have perfect love in your heart, it will drive out your fears and worries, your angers and jealousies, your failures and guilts, and make you a well-balanced and happy person.

In other words, Saint John says the only way to destroy our sickening emotions is developing our healing emotions.

Jesus tells the story (Matthew 24:14–30) of a man who had three servants. Before the man left on a long journey, he gave to one of his servants five talents, to another two, and to another one. Two of the servants invested their talents in such a way as to double them.

But the third servant did not use his. When the man returned, he highly complimented the two servants who did so well. But he had harsh words indeed for the servant who did nothing. In explaining his failure, the servant said, "I was afraid" (v. 25).

One of our most sickening fears is that fear of failure. That fear has made invalids out of many healthy people.

We have made success one of our gods, and we fall down and worship before it. Parents are often overly ambitious for their children. Not having reached the goals in life they desired, they relive those ambitions in their children, seeking a vicarious satisfaction as the child succeeds.

And many children have been driven into this paralyzing fear of failure. I have talked with people who were afraid to attempt even the simplest undertakings. Often you find that parents or teachers ridiculed them as children for even the smallest of failures. Many children have had this fear instilled in them by being unfavorably compared with more brilliant or capable children.

That is always the wrong approach. A person hungers for appreciation just as he hungers for bread, and without appreciation, no person can be his best. Some people think that if you compliment a person it will make him conceited. That is not true.

Look into your own heart and you will see that expressed appreciation makes you humble, never conceited. But because our hunger for appreciation is so great, if we do not receive it from others, we will bestow it upon ourselves. We will praise and magnify ourselves, and self-conceit is the result. Conversely, when this basic hunger for appreciation is received from others, one becomes truly humble.

A friend of mine tells of a boy who was a problem child from the time he was in the first grade. Almost every teacher he had assumed he was a hopeless case. It was discovered the boy's parents had a cruel tendency to find fault. The boy was beaten, shouted at, and ridiculed for his mistakes. At sixteen the boy had quit school and he went to work for the manager of an amusement park.

The manager was not a trained psychologist, but he did have a kind, understanding heart. He was a man of love, and it was natural for him to praise and thank the boy for each job which he did well. Little by little the boy quit thinking of failure as he began receiving the one thing for which his heart had been longing.

A little appreciating love cast out his fear.

I have the case histories of two women who had almost identical operations. One of the women was a shy, sensitive, overprotected person. The operation was very successful, but the lady was constantly depressed. She talked constantly of "the terrible thing" which had happened to her. She talked about how she would never be able to take care of herself. Three or four weeks after the operation she died.

As far as the operation was concerned, the case of the other woman was the same. However, her operation had been postponed until her baby was born. Her operation was performed two weeks later. In two more weeks, she was at home, and soon she was completely recovered.

She had no time to lie around a hospital and pamper herself. She had a baby, and that baby needed her. The deepest feeling she had was her love for that baby. I cannot write a definition of perfect love, but the love of a mother for her baby is the best example of perfect love that I know. Her love cast out all her fears about herself, and instead of dying, as did the first woman, she quickly was healed.

There was a girl who was brought to a hospital and died within a short time. Following the autopsy, the physician said to the girl's mother, "We could find no cause of death." The mother replied, "Oh, doctor, you don't have to tell me why she died. She died of a broken heart. The young man to whom she was engaged was killed a few weeks ago. Since that time she has had no interest in anything."

Of a broken heart. That means she had lost her love. Very often, the loss of love means the loss of security, maybe the loss of self-respect. Frequently when love is crushed, one becomes overwhelmed with the feeling of being not needed or not wanted. And that can be and often is fatal. It can destroy in a person any desire to live, and consciously or subconsciously that person begins to desire death. The desire for death becomes stronger than the instinct for self-preservation. Thus one *does* die of a broken heart.

The cure: Jesus said, ". . . he that loseth his life for my sake shall find it" (Matthew 10:39). Or again, ". . . seek ye first the kingdom of God, and his righteousness; and all these things shall be added unto you" (Matthew 6:33).

That is, when you give yourself to something greater than yourself, when some great cause becomes more important than your own life, and to that cause you give all of your interests and feelings, then that cause will give back to you a stronger and healthier life than you ever experienced before.

Self-centeredness makes us sick. Perfect love heals us.

Abraham Lincoln and his law partner, William Herndon, were arguing the question of whether or not any person ever performs a completely unselfish act. They were riding together through the country and came upon a pig caught in a rail fence. Herndon pretended not to see the animal and passed on by.

But Lincoln stopped, got down and waded through a muddy ditch, pulled the rails apart and released the pig.

Herndon pointed triumphantly to Lincoln's muddy shoes and spattered trousers, saying, "You see now I am right. Men are capable of performing unselfish deeds."

"Oh no," replied Lincoln, "if I had left that pig in the fence, I would have worried about him all night. I would have been so busy wondering if someone had rescued him, or if he was still held between those rails, that I would have lost my sleep. For my own peace of mind, I had to rescue the animal. So, you see, I was merely being selfish."

Without entering the argument of Lincoln and Herndon as to whether or not a person is capable of performing a completely unselfish act, that story does illustrate the fact that failure to give may sometimes be very costly. In Lincoln's case, it would have cost him a night's sleep and his peace of mind.

"For God so loved the world that He gave. . . ." Love is a process of giving. In fact, love demands expression, and if it is not expressed, it becomes a poison for one's own soul.

But in order to have love come into our lives, first we must express our love for others. "The song is to the singer, and comes back most to him; The gift is to the giver, and comes back most to him; The love is to the lover, and comes back most to him."

". . . With what measure ye mete, it shall be measured unto you . . ." said Jesus (Mark 4:24). Again, He said, "Give, and it shall be given unto you . . ." (Luke 6:38).

". . . perfect love casteth out fear . . ." says Saint John (1 John 4:18). What is the basis of fear? I think it is the possibility of losing—losing health, security, friends, or any of many things. If you have nothing to lose, then you have nothing to fear.

Perfect love gives without thought of return. Therefore, love has nothing to lose. Love has already given all that it has. Thus, love has nothing to fear. Love does cast out fear.

26

You Can Stake Your Life on Love

"For God so loved . . ." —that is the greatest statement in the Bible (John 3:16). It is the revelation of the character of God, the explanation of the laws that control the world in which we live, and the foundation upon which every successful life must be built.

No wonder the Bible warns us that even though one might have marvelous gifts and graces, talents and wealth, if that person does not have love, he is nothing. And, even though one might do many wonderful things and even give his life in service, there is no profit in such a life, unless that person possesses love (1 Corinthians 13:1–3). Love, and love alone, determines any person's worth and any person's success in this business of living. Love is the most important thing in life.

You may not understand much of the Bible. You may not be able to quote the Apostle's Creed or even the Lord's Prayer. You may have become the victim of sin. Your mind might be filled with doubt and despair. Even in spite of those things, you are still within the reach of God. But if you ever reach the point of killing all the love in your heart, then you become a pitiful creature, most miserable and without hope.

On the other hand, you may have an educated mind, give your talents in many worthwhile services, rise to places of prominence in the eyes of other people, live an honorable and decent life, but even after you have done all these things, if you have left love out of your life, you are a useless person and life for you is a failure. The absence of love is the explanation of the unhappiness and restlessness of vast multitudes of people today. Love is the one quality of character—the only one—about which we can say, "If a person has this, his life is good—without this, no matter what else he may have or do, life is bad."

EROS

What is love? That word has been used to describe so many things that we have become confused as to its real meaning. The Greeks had a word, *eros,* which we have translated as "love." Within the meaning of that word is the act of possessing. It really isn't love, rather is it a perversion of love.

For example, a young man falls in love with a girl. He then wants her entirely for himself. He thinks in terms of making her his. At first, he wants to go steady. That means she must not go with another boy. He wants to hold her close to himself. He wants to make her his wife. For him, that is not love, it is possessing.

Read again Shakespeare's *Othello.* He loved his wife, Desdemona, simply because of what she meant to him. And when he decided she was unfaithful to him, he killed her. So often, when some person does not respond to our love, that love is changed into hatred, and instead of love, we seek or wish for that person some hurt or destruction.

We erroneously think of love in terms of the Greek word *eros,* which means possessing for our own good. We remember Jane Carlyle, wife of the great English writer. Some thought she did not love her husband; rather she wanted to be his wife because of his fame and what that would mean to her.

We remember how Scrooge in Dickens's *Christmas Carol* lost his sweetheart because of his love for gold. Today, we see men neglect their families and everything good and fine in life because of their love for success or position or power. At the very center of such love is self.

Right at this point, we see the fatal error of many people's interest in religion. We pretend we love God, but often it is with an ulterior motive. It isn't God we want—instead we want peace of mind, or power in life, or the answer to our prayers, or we want to escape hell, or we want God's providences. And, so often, when something upsetting happens to us, we turn away from our faith in bitter resentment.

Here is a parent whose child died. As a result, that parent becomes filled with self-pity, or resentment, or doubt, and becomes an altogether unlovely person. That parent did not truly love. Instead, it merely possessed.

AGAPE

But there is another word which we also translate as love. It is the word of the New Testament, *agape.* That love is never focused on oneself, but rather upon the object of love. Its meaning is not found in possessing, but in just the opposite—in giving. "For God so loved the world that he gave . . ." (John 3:16).

Why did God make this world? Why did He make me? I often have wondered why He made us. I have been a bother to Him, and time and again I have disappointed Him. The real answer to why He made any of us is not because of what we can do for Him but because of what He can do for us. We came not because of necessity, but because of love. A couple may have a baby because they are lonely and because life for them has grown stale and empty. They feel a baby will put back into their lives what they have lost. On the other hand, a couple may have a baby because they have so much to give and they are not satisfied until they do give. You can have a baby for what it can do for you, or for what you can do for the baby. God made us for what He can do for us. That is the true expression of love.

LAWS OF LOVE

Now—that leads me to the very heart of this matter of love. Because the world, and all that is within it, is an expression of the love of God, then we can be sure that the world is governed by the laws of love. And if we are to really find life in its truest and fullest meaning, we must follow the pathways of love.

Suppose you took a trip to Alaska in the middle of the winter. Would you carry the same clothes that you would carry to Florida in the summer—thin cotton shirts or dresses, open shoes, your bathing suit, and no overcoat? No—one must adjust himself to the climate in which he lives, otherwise he would not survive.

So one must adjust himself to the spiritual environment of his world. The same God who made our physical world also made our spiritual world. We know that if we eat arsenic, we will die. Yet, we foolishly forget that when we put into our lives hatred, jealousy, selfishness, resentments, unforgiving spirits and the like, we kill the spirit of God within us. This is what the Bible means when it says, ". . . the soul that sinneth, it shall die" (Ezekiel 18:4).

MAN'S REDEMPTION

Now I come to man's chief problem. Many have despaired of our race. Many people believe man is a hopeless creature, that he cannot be redeemed. We have come to believe that self-assertion is one of our basic instincts. Put your finger into the hand of a tiny baby, and it will hold tightly to it. And as one grows, that possessive instinct grows with him and becomes the chains of his life. His ambitions lie in taking care of himself, possessing the things he wants, obtaining security for himself, doing the things that bring him pleasure. Those ambitions, we know, eventually result in frustration, but we seem powerless to do anything about them. True love is the surrendering of our very selves, and that is something man is unable to do by the exercise of his own will power.

And therein lies the redemption of the cross of Christ. Read again the life story of Teresa. For forty years she had been a very practical person living for herself, taking care of herself, getting what she could for herself. Though she was living in a convent, still she was living for herself. But one day, she became different. It happened in a moment.

As she walked along a hallway, she saw a picture of the Lord being scourged. She must have seen that picture a hundred times, but this time she saw it as she had never seen it before. She saw God suffering—suffering for love and for her. She fell on her knees. She arose a new soul. She said she arose with "a sense of unpayable debt," and all the balance of her life was different.

In many forms, and sometimes even in the most unlikely moments, that experience may come. We have gone along our self-seeking ways. We have known about Christ but we have never really seen Him. And then it happens, and we know what it means to be redeemed by His blood. Then we realize that His way is *the* Way. Instead of ourselves, He becomes the center of life for us. To Him we give ourselves, and we begin to walk the pathway of true love. Then we find life.

STAKED HIS LIFE ON LOVE

When one really loves God, then no sacrifice for God becomes too great.

Look at Henry Martyn, who has been called the "most heroic figure in the English Church since the time of Queen Elizabeth I." After a brilliant career at Cambridge, he heard the call to the mission field and tossed aside half a dozen possible careers to answer that call. He prepared himself for India in a spirit of complete dedication.

Then something else happened. He fell deeply in love with a girl named Lydia. He told her of his love for her and also of his orders from heaven. Would she go with him? Together, they could do great things for God.

She would not go. If he stayed in England, she would marry him. If he went to India, he must go alone. So the question hammered in his brain: "India or Lydia? Lydia or India?"

He chose aright. He went to India, and he went alone. He never again knew such love as he had known for Lydia. She married someone else and forever was beyond his love. For the remainder of his life there was the burden of that disappointment. Yet in the midst of that pain he said, "My dear Lydia and my duty called me different ways. Yet God hath not forsaken me. I am born for God only. Christ is nearer to me than father or mother, or sister." And I am sure he could have added, "Than Lydia, either."

There was a man who staked his life on love—love that thinks not of itself or what it can gain, but love which thinks only of what it can give. Would you say that in the end he won or that he lost?

I say it reverently and prayerfully, but God also staked His life on love. "For God so loved the world, that he gave his only begotten Son . . ." (John 3:16). I know He suffered and died because He followed the course of love, but would you say that in the end God won or that He lost?

The choice of Henry Martyn or the choice of Christ's cross does not often come to many Christians—yet, usually we face the choice to some degree. To follow the pathway of God's love may mean the giving up of this possession, or that pleasure, or the rendering of this service, or walking in this way of life.

Sometimes the choice boils down to simply: If I follow the pathway of love, I must take the chance of not living for myself, but living for Him. Can I afford to take that chance? Or must I first put my own needs and interest? And I answer that with the assurance, you *can* afford to stake your life on love.

27

Love—the Foundation of the Family

Jesus told a story about two men who built houses. One built his house on a rock—a firm foundation. The other built on the sand—a very *unfirm* foundation. Both houses got along fine for a time, but then the rains descended, the floods came, and the winds blew. The house on the rock stood: the house on the sand fell (Matthew 7:24–27).

To begin with, that simple story illustrates the need of building a house on a firm foundation. But we need to go beyond that. Also, we need a firm foundation for the home which we plan to put into our houses. A house can be washed away in a flood, blown away by a tornado, burned up by a fire. It is bad for a house to be destroyed.

But even worse is for a *home* to be destroyed—and homes can be destroyed by so many enemies:

Disagreements over money is one thing that can destroy a home.

Conflicts with one's in-laws can also destroy a home. Ever so often, I have heard someone say, "I married him; I did not marry his family." But that is not true. When one marries another person, he or she marries that other person's family also, and any other idea can bring trouble.

Different interests or a lack of common interest is something else that can destroy a home.

Failure of adjustments in the intimate marriage relation can also be fatally damaging.

Disagreements over children can shake a home's foundations.

Husbands and wives can lose their tempers.

Harsh words can be spoken, and the home foundations go crumbling down.

Alcohol and dope can be the basis of a home-destroying storm.

Religion is one of the foundations of a home, but religious differences can make that foundation crack.

Sooner or later, just like every house must face up to some storm, every home will also have its storms to face.

The sad truth is more than half the homes fail to survive. When a home falls, not only are the marriage partners hurt, often children and others are scarred for life.

There are many foundations of a home, but here let us concern ourselves with the one foundation which is the most important—and that is love. In fact, if a home has this foundation and no other, it still has a good chance for survival. But, it can have all other foundations and lack this foundation of love and fall into destruction.

Once a man consulted a psychiatrist about the best thing he could do for his children. He had made a list, including such things as: providing material necessities, such as food, clothes, house, and all the others; assuring an opportunity for education; making available religious training; instilling in the children proper social attitudes; setting a good moral example.

The psychiatrist said, "All these are extremely important, but you have not named the most important thing you can do for your children."

The man wondered aloud what was more important than the things he had named.

"The best thing you can do for your children," replied the psychiatrist, "is love their mother."

I think that is a wise statement, because children are alive to the kind of affection there is between father and mother. Nothing gives them a deeper sense of security than to know their parents love each other. Nothing shakes them quite as much as to realize love is lacking between the two adults they depend on the most.

One of the ministers I have loved and appreciated the most across the years has been Dr. Pierce Harris, who is now in the Father's House. When I first started in the ministry, I heard him preach. He captured me that day, and I've looked up to him ever since. For more than twenty-five years, he was pastor of the First Methodist Church in Atlanta, Georgia. Great multitudes of people were inspired by his ministry.

I shall never forget one night while I was living in Atlanta, Georgia. It was about one o'clock in the morning. A man from a radio station phoned to tell me that Dr. and Mrs. Harris had been in an automobile wreck, and that she was killed. I asked him where it happened, and he told me near Eatonton, Georgia. It was about seventy miles away. I hurriedly dressed and drove down there and located the hospital. I went quietly into his room, thinking he might be asleep. He was lying there in pain, but wide awake. As I came in the door, he said, "Charles, you ought not to have come down here tonight—but I knew you would come." I sat with him until daylight, and I shall always cherish those hours in my memory.

We used to travel a lot together to various preaching missions. One of my greatest joys was playing golf with him. He was a very outstanding golfer, and, as we would drive through the country, or walk around some golf course, we used to talk a lot about sermons. He had keen insight and deep wisdom, and from him I gained so much.

Once I had noticed that his subject for the next Sunday was: "Impressions That Make Life Impossible." That subject intrigued me, and that afternoon on the golf course, as we walked down the first fairway, I asked him about his sermon. He said, "I have four points in that sermon, and when we get to the end of the ninth hole, as we drink a Coca-Cola, I will tell you what they are." I agreed to that, and with some difficulty waited until we had finished nine holes. As we sat resting a few moments, I asked him to give me the "four impressions that make life impossible." As he began telling them to me, I wrote them on the back of our score card. I shall always prize that card. Here they are:

(1) The poisonous impression that only the present is important. He talked a little bit about people who never plan for tomorrow.

(2) The fatal impression that failure is final. He pointed out that one of the chief purposes of preaching was to put hope back into the hearts of those who have lost it. I remember, he said, "We need to encourage people to believe that one broken dream is not the end of dreaming."

(3) The dumb impression that drinking isn't dangerous. It was said of Jesus, "The sinners heard him gladly." Dr. Harris was that kind of a man. Many people whose lives had been shattered by liquor and other things came to hear him.

After he had talked about these three impressions that make life impossible, he said, "The fourth is the worst of all." Naturally, I was interested to hear what it was. He got up and said, "Come on, let's finish our golf game, and I will give you that last one when we get into the club house." I really did not enjoy the game as much after that because I was so interested in what the last one might be. After we got into the locker room, we sat down on a bench, and I said, "Now give me that last impression that makes life impossible." He told me:

> (4) The brutal impression that hearts cannot be broken. He said that love is a restless thing, and it seeks constant expression. He told me, "Love is the most delicate flower that grows in the garden of the heart, and it must be carefully cultivated."

Something else he said that day that I put down: "Love never dies; it has to be killed, but it can be killed."

I'll never forget that conversation with Dr. Pierce Harris, along with many, many others that we had.

I heard about a man who had what many would say was a rather peculiar habit. For years, he had a special date with his wife every Thursday night. He would come home in the afternoon, shave and shower, put on his best suit, and go out and get in his car and leave. In a little while, he would come back and ring the front doorbell. His wife would greet him at the door, and they would sit for a while in the living room and talk. Then they would go out to dinner and a show together. They would drive up to the front; he would escort her to the door, kiss her goodnight, and then go drive his car into the garage and come in through the back door.

It sounds sort of silly for a man to do that with his wife—but when that man died, his wife watered his grave with tears.

Falling in love is easy—but *staying* in love has to be worked at.

The other day I turned on the radio in my car and I heard

a man singing as he was picking a banjo. The title of one of his songs was, "When the Honeymoon Is Over, the Humdrum of Life Begins." That is the trouble, and that is why a lot of homes crumble and fall. If we expect to keep love alive, we must keep going through the motions of love.

For twenty years now, I have preached each Sunday on television. Many write in and say, "I am a shut-in." They may be old, crippled, or sick. Many of these cannot get out much, and have to stay in the house most of the time.

I have visited and spoken in quite a large number of jails and penitentiaries. It makes me sad to see men and women shut in behind prison bars.

Above most anything else, we Americans want freedom. We do not want to be shut-ins. Young people crave the chance to live their own lives. Women fight for their rights. Husbands or wives do not want to be dominated by the other. We do not want our nation to be governed by a dictator. We want to be free.

But I want to tell you something worse than being a shut-in—that is being a "shut-out."

Some young person may feel restricted by the rules of the parents in the home—but it would be far worse to be an orphan and to have no parents, or to be driven out of the home and not allowed to return.

A husband may feel that his wife is unreasonable and unpleasant and hard to live with—but go back and read Tennyson's story of Enoch Arden. He was considered dead, and his wife married again. He returned home and looked through the window to see his wife with her new husband. The balance of his days, he was a shut-out.

A man may complain about his government and high taxes, but then we remember the man without a country, who was not allowed to be a citizen anywhere.

Love is the opposite of being shut out. Love means acceptance—love means belonging. Love becomes the most important thing in life.

Today we hear a lot about the needs of children and young people. They need a lot of things, such as being listened to and hearing their side, learning what they are thinking about. They need discipline, but discipline is not enough. One of my best friends wrote these words: "I can remember when mother used to get after us boys. She would take me in the bedroom and talk to me. She would leave me sitting on the edge of the bed, but as she would go out of the room, she would turn around and say, 'But, son, remember I love you.' That meant more to me than any other thing in my life."

A lot of times children feel shut out. Their parents have not made them feel they were loved. The greatest tragedy is for a child or a youth to feel unwanted and unneeded and unloved.

I talked to a mother just recently whose teenage daughter is in trouble. She is not married; she is going to have a baby. The mother said a lot of harsh and bitter things to her. She talked about their family's being disgraced. I finally said to the mother, "You stop saying all those bitter things. That girl is hurt enough. You go home and tell that girl, and keep telling her many times every day, that you love her, that you are standing by her, that you are going to help her all the way through." I told that mother, "If you do not love your daughter now, she will likely never need your love again."

When Jesus wanted people to understand what God is like, He told them about a father who welcomed his prodigal son back home. Instead of fussing at the boy, the father ". . . fell on his neck and kissed him" (Luke 15:20).

There are some other foundations a home needs, but if we have love—real love—the other foundations will take care of themselves. Without love, no other foundations are strong enough.

CHRISTIAN HERALD ASSOCIATION AND ITS MINISTRIES

CHRISTIAN HERALD ASSOCIATION, founded in 1878, publishes The Christian Herald Magazine, one of the leading interdenominational religious monthlies in America. Through its wide circulation, it brings inspiring articles and the latest news of religious developments to many families. From the magazine's pages came the initiative for CHRISTIAN HERALD CHILDREN'S HOME and THE BOWERY MISSION, two individually supported not-for-profit corporations.

CHRISTIAN HERALD CHILDREN'S HOME, established in 1894, is the name for a unique and dynamic ministry to disadvantaged children, offering hope and opportunities which would not otherwise be available for reasons of poverty and neglect. The goal is to develop each child's potential and to demonstrate Christian compassion and understanding to children in need.

Mont Lawn is a permanent camp located in Bushkill, Pennsylvania. It is the focal point of a ministry which provides a healthful "vacation with a purpose" to children who without it would be confined to the streets of the city. Up to 1000 children between the ages of 7 and 11 come to Mont Lawn each year.

Christian Herald Children's Home maintains year-round contact with children by means of an *In-City Youth Ministry.* Central to its philosophy is the belief that only through sustained relationships and demonstrated concern can individual lives be truly enriched. Special emphasis is on individual guidance, spiritual and family counseling and tutoring. This follow-up ministry to inner-city children culminates for many in financial assistance toward higher education and career counseling.

THE BOWERY MISSION, located at 227 Bowery, New York City, has since 1879 been reaching out to the lost men on the Bowery, offering them what could be their last chance to rebuild their lives. Every man is fed, clothed and ministered to. Countless numbers have entered the 90-day residential rehabilitation program at the Bowery Mission. A concentrated ministry of counseling, medical care, nutrition therapy, Bible study and Gospel services awakens a man to spiritual renewal within himself.

These ministries are supported solely by the voluntary contributions of individuals and by legacies and bequests. Contributions are tax deductible. Checks should be made out either to CHRISTIAN HERALD CHILDREN'S HOME or to THE BOWERY MISSION.

Administrative Office: 40 Overlook Drive, Chappaqua, New York 10514
Telephone: (914) 769-9000